The Spirit of the Forty-Second

Narrative of the
42nd Battalion, 11th Infantry Brigade,
3rd Division,
Australian Imperial Forces,
during the
Great War, 1914-1918

Written and Compiled by
VIVIAN BRAHMS

The Naval & Military Press Ltd

Published by
The Naval & Military Press Ltd
5 Riverside, Brambleside, Bellbrook
Industrial Estate, Uckfield, East Sussex,
TN22 1QQ England
Tel: +44 (0) 1825 749494
Fax: +44 (0) 1825 765701
www.naval-military-press.com
www.military-genealogy.com
www.militarymaproom.com

In reprinting in facsimile from the original, any imperfections are inevitably reproduced and the quality may fall short of modern type and cartographic standards.

Honours and Distinctions

★

42nd Battalion, A.I.F.

NUMBER ON NOMINAL ROLLS

Discharged	2,410
Killed in Action, Died of Wounds or Sickness	544
TOTAL	**2,954**
Wounded	1,130
Wounded Twice	254
Wounded Three Times	53
Wounded Four Times	13
Prisoners of War	2

Decorations Awarded

Military Medals	90
M.M.'s with Bar	5
D.C.M.'s	12
Military Crosses	22
D.S.O.'s	5
M.S.M.'s	4
Croix de Guerre	4
Mentioned in Despatches	9
TOTAL	**151**

First Published 1938.

Made and Published
in Brisbane, Australia.
[All Rights Reserved]

42nd BATTALION, A.I.F.

under the command of

Lt.-Colonel A. R. WOOLCOCK,
D.S.O., C. de G.

•

BATTLE HONOURS ALLOTTED TO THE
42nd BATTALION, A.I.F.

GREAT WAR, 1914–1918

MESSINES, 1917; YPRES, 1917;
BROODSEINDE, PASSCHENDAELE,
SOMME, 1918; ANCRE, 1918,
HAMEL, AMIENS,
MONT ST. QUENTIN, HINDENBURG LINE

Administrative Officers, Company Commanders, etc.

★

Battalion Commander:
LT.-COLONEL A. R. WOOLCOCK

Seconds In Command:
MAJORS J. FARRELL, E. J. DIBDIN

Adjutants:
MAJOR E. J. DIBDIN, CAPTAINS R. F. PICKERING, A. P. ST. JOHN, G. DUNBAR, W. H. McDONNELL, LIEUTENANT A. C. DIBDIN

Quartermaster:
CAPTAIN L. W. C. ANDERSON

Medical Officers:
CAPTAINS G. H. CAMERON, E. G. THOMSON, MAJOR J. HARDIE, CAPTAIN G. M. FAITHFULL

Lewis Gun Officers:
CAPTAIN J. FINLAY, LIEUTENANTS E. A. CARR, J. L. TARDENT

Signalling Officers:
LIEUTENANTS H. W. M. BULL, C. S. TRUDGIAN, C. V. M. BROOM, E. E. PATERSON

Intelligence Officers:
CAPTAIN G. DUNBAR, LIEUTENANTS D. FRASER, C. W. C. O'CONNELL, J. L. TARDENT

Transport Officers:
LIEUTENANTS C. T. O. SHEPHERD, H. A. R. SQUIRES

Chaplains:
MAJOR T. P. WOOD, CAPTAIN H. W. JONES

Company Commanders:

A Company—
CAPTAINS T. MILLS, R. S. RANKIN, MAJOR A. C. MOYES, CAPTAINS J. FINLAY, S. WARRY

B Company—
CAPTAINS A. POTT, A. P. ST. JOHN, LIEUTENANT F. C. LEWIS, T./CAPTAIN C. S. TRUDGIAN

C Company—
MAJOR A. HERON, CAPTAINS J. LEAHY, T. JACK, W. H. A. McDONNELL

D Company—
MAJOR C. C. CAMPBELL, CAPTAINS D. BINNIE, C. CAMERON, A. W. HALSTEAD, E. YELLAND, R. F. O'BRYEN

Preface

•

THE story of the 42nd Battalion which I have compiled is the result of labours spread over a series of many years.

There has ever been a demand for a "History" of Our Battalion, but beyond getting a copy of its records, which I extracted from the records of the 11th Infantry Brigade, the loan of which was obtained in 1925 from the Defence Authorities, through the kind services of Colonel E. J. Dibdin, no progress could be reported from year to year.

Some considerable time ago a "History Committee" was formed, which after going carefully into ways and means, decided that no funds being available for the purpose, the compilation of a comprehensive printed history was an impossibility. Rather than allow the years to pass without making at least an effort to preserve the traditions and deeds of the Battalion, it was recommended that steps be taken to obtain a typewritten copy of its achievements to hand down to posterity along with the Memorial Board containing the names of our Illustrious Dead. It was proposed that this history should be as concise as the relation of so vast a number of important exploits would render possible.

The first attempt to get something of a concrete nature was to allot to certain members of the Battalion a particular portion of the writing dealing with the period in which they were intimately acquainted with the Battalion and its work. The response was unfortunately disappointing, and it appeared that the matter of a 42nd Battalion history would again fall through. At length, rather than allow more years to accumulate, and having failed to unearth a writer of greater experience, I stepped into the breach and volunteered to carry out the compilation to the best of my ability. Extracts from the 11th Brigade records have been my main source of information, and I have since discovered that many of those records are the work of Lieut. Jules Tardent, Captain R. F. O'Bryen and others.

As it is now impossible to obtain details of every individual performance, many might be inadvertently omitted were I to attempt to give the names of those responsible for the carrying out of various movements and meritorious work, therefore, instead of endeavouring to do so, I have refrained from mentioning any names beyond those of our Battalion Commander and the first man killed in the War Zone.

During the early stages of writing I was greatly indebted to Sergt-Major W. J. Judd for the loan of his diary, which gave me an idea of the manner in which the work might be approached.

Starting so far back as 1925, I made fair progress until 1931, when I felt the task, after all, was beyond me, and I relinquished the writing. Six years elapsed, when in response to requests, encouragement, and a sense of duty, I felt the urge to complete my unfinished work. I made another attempt, and now at last, after thirteen years, the book is ready for publication.

I desire to acknowledge the wonderful assistance rendered by Colonel E. J. Dibdin, without whose aid this publication would have been an impossibility. Besides furnishing details of the early days of the Battalion, his help has been invaluable.

Information regarding the various attempts to extinguish the Battalion have been supplied me by Mr. George Brigham, whilst Lt. R. D. Fisher and Mr. Verdi Schwinghammer have imparted some valuable hints.

I desire to stress the sympathetic encouragement accorded me by Captain A. C. Dibdin, and last, but by no means least, the greatest encouragement of all, at the hands of the Battalion Commander, Colonel A. R. Woolcock, who states he wholeheartedly approves of the manner in which our story has been told, namely, from the point of view of the man in the ranks, without attempting to discuss matters of tactics or strategy.

My thanks and appreciation are due to all members of the present "History Committee," namely, Captain A. C. Dibdin, Messrs. George Brigham, Andy Burnett, Charles H. Green, Arthur Gallagher, Frank Marrian, George Angell, and Sergt.-Major W. J. Judd, and to all members of the 42nd Battalion A.I.F., who have helped to make this publication a possibility.

VIVIAN BRAHMS.

Brisbane, June 6th, 1938.

Patriotism and Duty

Formation—Training—Embarkation—England.

Birth and Infancy

Towards the end of 1915, the Defence Authorities decided to form a new division of the Australian Imperial Forces; Queensland was called upon to provide two battalions.

It was about Christmas time that sites were selected. Thompson's Paddock, at Enoggera, some few miles distant from Brisbane, was allotted to what was at first called "The 36th Battalion," which soon afterwards became permanently altered to "The 42nd." Its Commanding Officer was Lt.-Colonel A. R. Woolcock, who remained the Battalion Commander until the end.

Then ensued the preparation of rolls, attestation-papers, allotments and pay-books. Issues of clothing and equipment followed in due course. Spasmodic training, fatigue duties and the furnishing of picquets, vaccination and innoculations, gradually eliminated the civilian side of life from the embryo soldier.

As the weeks passed by, signallers, transport, bands, and headquarters staff and so forth, were evolved, until at daybreak on June the 3rd, 1916, the 42nd Battalion marched out of Thompson's Paddock to the railway station at Enoggera Rifle Range. Thence it proceeded, in three trains, to Sydney, where it arrived at 5.30 p.m. next day.

Embarkation upon the s.s. "Borda" then took place at Wooloomooloo. The transport drew out and anchored in Rushcutter's Bay. Next day, whilst at anchor, motor launches in dozens surrounded the "Borda," the occupants waving and sending messages and receiving replies. Some of these replies after being written on paper, were placed in a slit made in a raw potato, to ensure a safer passage when thrown through the air. The "Borda" sailed at 11.0 a.m. that day, and then, as Sydney Heads were passed half an hour later, we said "Good-bye" to Australia.

EARLY SIGNS OF THE 42nd's INITIATIVE

Before leaving Thompson's Paddock, the men of the 42nd Battalion gave evidence of the spirit of "initiative" which later on proved to be one of the characteristics of the Battalion. Only ten per cent. of those in camp were allowed "leave" each night, but it could not be denied that the remaining 90 per cent. were dissatisfied to remain in camp, consequently there was always a large proportion nightly absent without leave.

On one occasion a particularly zealous officer determined to make "examples" of these defaulters and set a trap to capture them. He knew they would return by the last train from Brisbane which also brought back to camp the City Picquet, which the 42nd Battalion had to furnish to patrol the streets of Brisbane. This officer had sentries posted at all entrances to the camp, and had everything in readiness to catch those who were "A.W.L."

The train was heard to arrive at Enoggera Station, and about twenty minutes later the steady and regular crunch of marching troops was heard. The officer in charge of the body was heard cautioning the men to "March to Attention." Then warning them to put out cigarettes, and to watch their step. A well ordered column of 50 men or more marched into camp to the command of "City Picquet—Right Wheel." Then came the order: "City Picquet—Halt! Right Turn." Then followed the caution: "Now you fellows, don't make a noise getting into your bunks. Remember there are men trying to sleep. Dis-miss."

When they had all turned in, the conscientious officer sat back and awaited the arrival of the "birds" who were absent without leave. He had not long to wait before a second body of troops, 50 or more strong, marched orderly into Camp to the command of—"City Picquet, Right Wheel." This second body was the REAL City Picquet. The others were the defaulters.

THE BATTALION'S FIRST CASUALTY

Whilst steaming through the Red Sea our first

BEFORE AND AFTER

Top Illustration depicts 42nd Battalion in training at Enoggera, 1916.

Lower Illustration shows the Battalion marching through a French Village, 1918.

casualty was sustained. One of the boys died from pneumonia and was buried at sea with full naval and military honours.

INNOCULATED AGAIN IN EGYPT

Suez was reached on July 6th, and next day we arrived at Tel-el-Kebir in Egypt, where we remained for a few days and thus gave the doctor an opportunity to diligently exploit his prowess with "The Needle," and so, the 42nd was once more innoculated.

INNOCULATED AGAIN ON THE TRANSPORT

The voyage was continued on the "Borda," on which we re-embarked at Alexandria, for the passage through the Mediterranean.

The doctor, who was termed in military phraseology, the M.O. (Medical Officer), but by the troops familiarly dubbed—"The Quack," had heard some mention of the word "Cholera." This was the signal to again bring forth the needle. We were lined up. Sleeves were rolled up. A patch of iodine. A stab. And once again the 42nd Battalion was innoculated.

WE ARRIVE AT, AND PASS THROUGH FRANCE

The menace of enemy submarines was very great, but we reached Marseilles, in Southern France, without mishap on July the 19th. We proceeded through France by train to Le Havre. It was here that we first saw a Red Cross train. Painted all white with large crosses of red, occupied by wounded men and nurses, it was the means of making us realise how near we were getting to the battlefield, and how grim was the job we had on hand.

WE ARRIVE IN ENGLAND

We crossed the English Channel on the night of July the 22nd, and disembarked next morning at Southampton, travelling thence to Amesbury by train. We eventually reached our new home on July the 23rd. Our address for the next three months was Number 11 Camp, Larkhill, Salisbury Plain. We spent this time steadily acquiring the arts of war and assiduously training both body and mind for that great day when we should meet the enemy face to face.

On September the 27th, the Third Australian Division, of which we were a unit, was reviewed by His Majesty King George the Fifth. Including New Zealand troops, there was a parade of 38,500 men. It was a most inspiring sight.

The largest number of troops that we had ever seen on a route march was on the occasion when the entire Third Division, consisting of 18,000 men, with vehicles, animals, and mechanical transport passed along the roads stretching many miles around Salisbury Plain. The display was spectacular and impressive. This took place on November 13th, twelve days prior to our embarkation for France.

THE 11th BRIGADE OF THE 3rd DIVISION A.I.F.

The 11th Infantry Brigade to which we belonged consisted of two Battalions of Queenslanders, the 41st and the 42nd; one Battalion of South Australians, the 43rd; and a Western Australian Battalion, the 44th.

The other infantry brigades of the Third Division were the 9th and 10th. The former contained all New South Wales Units, whilst the latter was made up of Victorian Units with the exception of the 40th Battalion which was composed mainly of Tasmanians.

It might here be mentioned that many Queensland Units contained men from the Northern Rivers of New South Wales, which was part of our military district.

COLOUR PATCHES

The Colour Patches of the Third Divisional troops, worn at the top of either sleeve of both tunics and overcoats were oval in shape and made in two colours. The bottom colour represented the brigade and the top colour designated the unit. The Brigade colours were: The Ninth, Green; The Tenth, Red; The Eleventh, Saxe Blue. The Battalion Colours went in rotation, the same in each brigade, as follows: Black, Dark Blue, Brown, White. Hence the colour patches of the Third Division were:—

Ninth Brigade: 33rd, Black; 34th, Dark Blue; 35th, Brown; 36th, White. All worn above the brigade colour, Green.

Tenth Brigade: 37th, Black; 38th, Dark Blue; 39th,

Brown; 40th, White. All worn above the brigade colour, Red.

Eleventh Brigade: 41st, Black; 42nd, Dark Blue; 43rd, Brown; 44th, White. All worn above the brigade colour, Saxe Blue.

METHOD OF WEARING THE LARGE FELT HAT

During the time the Third Division was in training, the troops were distinguished from those of other Australian Divisions by the manner of wearing the felt hat. The Third Divvy Troops wore the hat with the brim turned down completely, the large rising sun badge being adjusted in the centre front, whilst the men of the other four Divisions wore their hats with the rising sun badge displayed on that part of the brim which was turned up at the left hand side, and this was the style that was subsequently adopted as uniform for all Australian Divisions.

THE TERM "EGGS-A-COOK"

Up to this time, the First, Second, Fourth, and Fifth Divisions had seen active service at Gallipoli and on the Somme. They had also done some training in Egypt, where the "Gyppo" vendors of fruit and chocolates advertised their wares by calling them "verra nice, verra sweet, verra clean. Two for One." (This meant, two of them for one half-piastre). They also sold hard-boiled eggs, in the same manner, calling out: "Eggs-a-cook. Verra sweet, verra clean. Two for one." When the Third Divisional troops appeared, with their turned down hats and their oval, or egg-shaped, colour patches, members of the other four "Fighting Divisions," as they called themselves, immediately yelled out: "Here they are. Eggs-a-cook. Verra nice, verra sweet, verra clean. Two for one." It may have started as a joke, but it unfortunately developed into a term of derision.

There was a little doggerel verse to the tune of "The Girl I Left Behind Me," which went:

"Oh, the First and the Second are in the line,
And the Fourth and Fifth are behind them.
But when we look, for the Eggs-a-cook,
I'm ———d if you can find them."

This, when sung in the hearing of men of the Third

Division, was usually the signal for a box-on or brawl, but that was before the Third Division had made a name for itself at Messines and Passchendaele, and later on with its greatest exploit of all, which gained for it unstinted praise and everlasting respect. This, was at the time the Germans broke through the British lines and the Fifth British Army was retreating in haste. Pushing on, to support our Fourth Division hanging on at Dernancourt, with but a mere handful of cavalry to act as support; without the aid of artillery other than four field guns, which were subsequently withdrawn, the derided Eggs-a-cook Division, between the Somme and the Ancre, bore the entire brunt of stopping that avalanche of victory-flushed enemy troops, swooping onwards towards Amiens.

Unflinchingly the Eggs-a-cooks withstood the onslaught, held the enemy at bay and snatched victory from his very jaws. But we are progressing too fast. We must return to Salisbury Plain, where our 42nd Battalion is still awaiting orders to proceed to The Front.

Adventure

Arrival in France—Baptism of Fire—Trench Warfare

Off to the Front. Departure from Salisbury Plain

Saturday, November 25th, 1916, witnessed the departure from Salisbury Plain of the 42nd Battalion.

After chafing for months under the routine of drill and exercise, the Battalion at last emerged as a smart, well-equipped, highly-trained fighting unit, with every man fit and eager to get to grips with the enemy. Its strength was 33 officers and 994 other ranks.

Reveille was sounded at 4.30 a.m. It was a cold bleak morning on which we partook of our last breakfast at Number 11 Camp, Larkhill. After the meal a period of tremendous hustle and bustle ensued. There was the strapping and unstrapping of equipment, the packing of packs, to say nothing of the unceasing struggles to get all personal possessions, gear, ammunition, rations, blankets and utensils securely buckled to our bodies. These weighed approximately 100 lbs., exclusive of rifles.

At length we fell in for final inspection, then off we went on the four-mile journey to Amesbury railway station, gaily marching to the strains of the "Colonel Bogey March," played by the Battalion Band. The skirl of the pipes also helped us along.

THE AUSTRALIAN BLACK WATCH

Our Battalion bore the same regimental number as the Highland Regiment called "The Black Watch," hence the 42nd Battalion A.I.F. was jocularly referred to as "The Australian Black Watch." A drum and pipe band always accompanied us. It may have been a coincidence, but we certainly did receive into our ranks, a number of men who were either born Scotsmen or of Scottish descent.

SOUTHAMPTON

The Battalion left Amesbury in three trains, which arrived at Southampton at 11 a.m., noon, and 2 p.m. respectively. Here in large sheds adjacent to the wharf we remained waiting for darkness to fall. It was not advisable for transports to cross the English Channel in daylight.

During the long hours that elapsed we consumed countless buns and cakes, vast quantities of chocolate, fruit, chew-gum and other kinds of edibles which were purchasable at the canteens in the sheds. We smoked countless cigarettes and drank every kind of liquid available. This was the only relief we got during the tedious and monotonous afternoon and evening.

At last the long weary wait came to an end and we gladly received, and cheerfully obeyed, the order to "Fall in." Embarkation on the Channel transports started at 8 p.m. and after a rough passage, Le Havre was reached the following morning (Sunday).

LE HAVRE REST CAMP

Disembarkation took place at midday amid a storm of rain and sleet. In spite of the weather, the French civilians turned out "en masse" to welcome us. We shouted in French, telling them that the War would soon be over, now that the 42nd had arrived, but the townsfolk just stared and made no reply. It seemed to us that they did not understand their own language.

A long trying hill at the end of a six-mile march ushered the Battalion into the "Rest Camp" (so-called).

What a desolate scene met our eyes. The ground oozed with mud, and rows of discoloured sodden tents stood there dripping and leaking, offering very dubious shelter. Our first night out from England was spent in an uninviting atmosphere of gloom and dejection.

OOTERSTEENE

It was with much pleasure that we left Le Havre early next morning. The march to the station was downhill and therefore a lot easier. We spent the next 30 hours travelling by train, in horse boxes, which were marked: "8 chevaux, 40 hommes." That meant the truck was supposed to accommodate either eight horses or forty men.

We reached Bailleul at 3 o'clock on Tuesday afternoon. Thence we marched to the village of Ootersteene. When we got there, we found the place wrapped in a dense mantle of fog. We had to wait some considerable time in the streets before billeting arrangements were completed.

It was fortunate for us that we had with us two brothers, each a proficient linguist. They acted as interpreters on many occasions and thus greatly facilitated smoothing out the difficulties which we occasionally got into with the French authorities and civilians. It was a novelty to us to find ourselves living in schools and halls, barns and out-houses, all more or less in a state of disrepair.

Five days were spent in Ootersteene, training and getting used to the unusual conditions. It was here that we were issued with our "Box-respirators," and drilled in the use of them. These were our protection from the gas used by the enemy. We looked a weird lot of objects with our faces completely encased in rubber masks, with glass-covered apertures to see through, obtaining our air through a snake-like tube attached to the respirator. The term "Box-respirator" was soon corrupted into "Gaspirator." It was here, too, that we embarked upon our serious attempts to master the French language. We also experienced our first "Pay-day" in the field, which enabled many a 42nd man to cultivate an appetite for "Egg and Chip Banquets," and a taste for Vin Blanc and Vin Rouge.

ARMENTIERES.

On December 6th Ootersteene was left behind and we marched thence through Bailleul on to Armentieres, arriving there late in the afternoon and were billeted at a cotton factory in Rue de la Paix with our headquarters in Rue Sadi Carnot.

Prior to the War, Armentieres was a hive of industry, containing factories of all descriptions, especially for weaving woollen, cotton and canvas goods. It is not possible to recall our early days spent in that town without visualising the scenes of intense activity which continued despite the fact that part of the town formed portion of our Front Line. Civilians carried on their various avocations, whilst cafes and estaminets reaped a rich harvest from the constantly arriving and departing troops. Little mademoiselles came round to our billets in the cold dark hours of the wintry mornings with cakes and cups of hot coffee, for which they charged us deux sous (two half-pennies), and the young boys, whom we called petits garcons, came as far as our subsiduary lines to sell us the daily papers.

We found the town badly knocked about, especially the churches, but considering its proximity to the front line certain parts were wonderfully intact.

Whilst here we made purchases of many kinds of fancy goods such as laces and silks, and elaborate post cards. There were many shops in the vicinity of the ruined Town Hall, which stood in a Square, designated by the troops as "Half-past Eleven Square," due to the fact that the hands of the Town Hall clock, which had been hit some months prior to our arrival, stopped at 11.30 and remained so. A few months later, Armentieres was bombarded by gas shells which forced the civilians to evacuate. The town was ultimately reduced to ruins.

Nowadays, when the name of Armentieres is mentioned, it brings to memory a fictitious French lady of whom songs of many versions have been sung. It is more than likely that future generations will smile at episodes that have been woven around the idiosyncrasies and character of "Mademoiselle from Armentieres."

OUR FIRST CASUALTY IN THE WAR ZONE

Although we found the town very quiet upon arrival, it was only three days later, on Sunday, December 10th, that we were startled by a sudden bombardment. It was during this shelling that our first casualty in the War Zone occurred. The first man killed in our Battalion was Sergeant Hannah, when standing near a church close to our billets.

THE BATH PARADE

General training continued assiduously, and now we were introduced to another active service institution, namely, the Bath Parade. Eight to twelve men were placed in parties. Each of these parties bathed together in large beer vats filled with hot water and disinfectant. When the bathers had been in the bath the allotted time, the attendant let in more and more hot water until the temperature was too high for any human being to endure. Changes of underclothing were issued prior to entering the bath. Meanwhile, tunics and breeches underwent fumigation and hot irons were pressed along the seams of the garments in order to kill the vermin, called "chats," and their eggs. Up to this time the Third Division was considered clean, but henceonwards it became as lousy as all the other Divisions.

INSPECTION BY THE COMMANDER-IN-CHIEF

On Friday, December 22nd, the 42nd Battalion with other units of the Third Division was inspected at Steenwerke by General Sir Douglas Haig, Commander-in-chief of the British Expeditionary Forces, who complimented the men upon their soldierly appearance and bearing.

OUR FIRST CHRISTMAS ON ACTIVE SERVICE

The following day, Saturday, December 23rd, fifty per cent. of the specialists, that is, machine-gunners, signallers, bombers, etc., of the 36th Battalion, then holding the line, were relieved by the same number of specialists of the 42nd Battalion. The rest of us made our initial entry into the front line trenches the next day.

In the early hours of the morning, before the dawn of Christmas Eve, under the cover of darkness, we stole silently across Half-past Eleven Square and Barbed-wire Square, which were enveloped in a blanket of snow. We were loaded up with full pack and equipment and went steadily on until a large red building was reached.

THE GUM-BOOT STORE

This was called "The Gum-boot Store."

Here every man was issued with a pair of rubber boots which had to be returned when the term in the trenches was over. These boots reached from the toes up to the thighs, and after a while, created a freezing sensation in the feet. They seemed to accumulate as much moisture as they were designed to keep out. This was due to the condensing of the perspiration from the body. Alongside of the Gum-boot Store was a Y.M.C.A. canteen, where tea and biscuits could be obtained prior to entering the trenches.

LUNATIC LANE

The system of trenches in front of Armentieres was eventually entered by a communicating trench called Lunatic Lane, so named after the Lunatic Asylum which stood at the head.

We experienced much difficulty getting through the trenches with our full packs and equipment, and an unauthorised blanket or two. Especially was this so when we met parties of troops coming from the opposite direction whom we had to pass. We, however, were learning. Ever afterwards, our packs and blankets were left at the Quartermaster's store prior to taking over the line, and they were called for again upon our relief.

CHRISTMAS EVE AND CHRISTMAS DAY, 1916

These two days were unexpectedly quiet.

A pleasing feature, and to us a great surprise, was to discover how exceedingly well the organisation of the Battalion was being maintained. The transport brought their limbers right up close to the firing line. Working and carrying parties, working forwards and backwards, like streams of ants, kept the troops supplied with ammunition, wire and all the necessities for carrying on warfare.

The comfort of the men was not neglected. The Battalion cooks, who were always referred to as "The Babbling Brooks," installed their travelling kitchens in the subsiduary lines. There were four of these cookers. One to each company. Throughout the day the cooks kept us supplied with hot food. There was tea, morning and evening, and stew at midday. These meals were brought up from the cooks by mess-orderlies who worked together in pairs. Strapped to the back of one of them was a large vacuum container filled with either stew or tea. These were always acceptable and generally quite hot.

The mess-orderlies also distributed the large Army biscuits, which we called "Anzac Wafers," on account of

HOUPLINES, FEBRUARY, 1917.

A Party starting out for the Line, wearing sheepskin vests, and cap-comforters underneath steel helmets covered with hessian from sandbags, leather trench gloves, "Gaspirators" and smiles.

their thickness and weight. They also brought round issues of cheese, tins of bully beef, jam and bread. The latter, when plentiful, would work out at a daily ration of "four men to a loaf." These commodities were carried around in sand bags, which had a way of shedding their jutey hairs on the contents. Especially did they spread themselves on the cheese and margerine, which was the name of the substitute for butter.

POSTAL ARRANGEMENTS

The postal arrangements were well administered. Our letters and parcels were delivered right up to the front line trenches. The regularity that was displayed by the transport and other quartermaster's details deserves to be recorded as an outstanding feature of excellent organisation.

GIFTS FROM THE AUSTRALIAN COMFORTS FUND

The distribution of gifts from the Australian Comforts Fund was greatly appreciated. This narrative would be incomplete did it not contain a reference to those splendid Australian women and girls, the mothers, wives, daughters, and sweethearts of the men who were fighting. It is fitting to record the manner in which they kept us supplied with comforts otherwise unobtainable.

Some of these parcels of comforts were delivered to us on Christmas Day and contained among other things, Christmas puddings. These were served up to us, steaming hot and in perfect condition. The parcels also contained tins of cocoa and milk, ready to be made hot at any time by the aid of blocks of composition containing mainly Benzoline, and known to us by the name of "Tommy Cookers." Besides these, there were fruit cakes, confectionery and tins of various delicacies. There were socks, gloves and cap-comforters, knitted by loving hands. These prevented the cold penetrating the extremities whilst large sheep-skin vests kept our bodies warm.

THE IMPORTANCE OF OUR FIRST EXPERIENCE IN THE TRENCHES

Although there is no record that shows that anything of outstanding importance occurred during this, our first term in the trenches, yet it was a period over which the Battalion had been subjected to a most serious and vital trial.

Officers and men alike had been put to the test. It was our initiation. All ranks from the Battalion Commander down to the lowliest private soldier had learnt what was likely to be expected of him, and how he might be called upon to act spontaneously in cases of emergency. Here we had received first-hand knowledge and insight into the workings of the military machine. Here we proved conclusively that our training had hardened us to withstand the rigours of intense cold and discomfort, and here it was that we learnt that it is possible to bear the deafening and demoralising roar of hostile artillery barrages unflinchingly and with unimpaired nerve.

Nightly our wiring parties and patrols climbed over the top to strengthen our defences and to learn what could be learnt about the enemy's.

It was during this period we experienced the eeriness of No-man's Land, got used to machine-gun bursts, to the "ping" of bullets, to the weird shadows moving up and down, backwards and forwards, as the enemy's star-shells rose and fell, and to the feeling that at any moment a hostile patrol might be encountered.

PARAPET JOE

We did our share of sniping and got in some good practice with our machine-guns.

There was one German machine-gunner who deserves to be remembered in these annals. He swept the parapet with precision, and at the same time amused us with his rhythm and syncopation. Although we never met him, we gave him a name and christened him "Parapet Joe."

NEW YEAR'S DAY, 1917.

On this day we were relieved in the trenches by the 44th Battalion, and assumed that we were out of the line for a while, but we had yet to learn of a military paradox that existed, namely:—

"When you are in the Line—you are in.

And when you are out of the Line—you are still in."

And so it was with us. No sooner were we relieved in the trenches than the entire Battalion was ordered back again employed as working parties.

WORKING PARTIES

A working party consisted of detachments of men sent out to perform certain laborious work, such as digging trenches and laying cables. There were also "carrying parties," for taking up to the front line barbed wire, duckboards, ammunition, etc. "Wiring parties" laid barbed wire entanglements in No-man's Land in front of our trenches. There were also "ration parties" for carrying rations and "burial parties.".

A working party might be under the supervision of an engineer and build railways and construct concrete dug-outs, or be directed by some pioneer officer in the reveting of trenches and the laying of duckboard tracks. They also built gun pits for the artillery and emplacements for the Stoke's Mortar Batteries.

Decidedly, the infantry was the "handmaiden" of all the technical units.

MORE 42nd INITIATIVE

It was in the performance of one of these tasks that the spirit of the Battalion's initiative again came to the fore.

The Brigade Staff was particularly fussy about certain details, such as the exact time the working party reported, the quantity of work performed, but most especially, the exact number of men who were detailed for the job.

Instinctively we learnt how to avoid difficulties and to observe the brewing of trouble. On one occasion a working party of one hundred was detailed to report to an engineer officer for the job of burying a cable. Only ninety-six men assembled. It was too cold to wait about for the other four stragglers, so the N.C.O. in charge marched them off and everyone thought all was well, until suddenly a Staff Officer was observed standing ready to check their numbers. Half the party marched by the officer and was counted, and then whilst he was busily engaged in checking the remainder, the four men who comprised the leading file doubled round the nearest street corner, re-joined the party at the rear and marched past as the last four, and thus made up the full complement.

L'EPINETTE SALIENT

Whilst at Armentieres we occupied a sector in the Houplines district called L'Epinette Salient, which was approached by trenches known as Quality Street and Willow Walk. The names of the communicating trenches to right, left and centre sectors were, respectively, Plank Avenue, Japan Road, and Second House Avenue.

The 42nd remained in this locality, until relieved by the 35th Battalion on March 11th. In the meantime the usual trench warfare continued, casualties occurred daily, whilst the weather was exceedingly rigorous; in fact, it was the coldest winter known in these parts for many years past.

SATURDAY AFTERNOON MINNIE STRAAF

On Saturday, January 20th our trenches were subjected to intense bombardment by Minenwerfer and high explosive shells, resulting in casualties to the extent of one officer shell-shocked and two killed and twelve wounded, other ranks. Among the miraculous escapes was that of a D Company man who was buried when a "Minnie" blew in his "gun possie," but was unearthed when another "Minnie" fell close by.

The first military medal awarded to the Battalion was earned this day.

"MINNIES"

One of the deadliest of trench-mortar bombs used against us was the "Minnenwerfer," more intimately known to us by the term "Minnie." These bombs exploded with a deafening noise and the concussion was nerve wracking. They were so large that it was possible to trace their progress through the air, although in the final descent their course was erratic. At night they appeared like large blood-red sticks in the sky.

In spite of the destruction they caused to life and defences and the demoralisation they were calculated to create, we at length became so used to them that we were able to await and meet the heaviest "Minnie Barrage" without getting panicky.

ENEMY RUSES AND BOOBY TRAPS

Several traps and ruses were discovered by our scouts. Apparently harmless looking objects were left about in order to entrap the unwary. They were given the name of "booby traps." Our scouts found a French tricolour flag flying from a staff in front of the enemy's wire entanglements. This was obviously a trap. They discovered the strings of three stick-grenades attached to the pole holding the flag in position. The grenades were made firm in the clay. The staff was surrounded by trip wire which was strewn over the only dry route. One of the scouts, however, by wading through four feet of water disconnected the grenades and brought back the flag in spite of enemy machine guns which were trained on the spot.

The same day a patrol discovered a fixed rifle trained on to a gap in the parapet. From this point intermittent fire was carried on during the night.

A few days later further trip-wire was discovered. Two special bombs were attached to this and these were in turn fastened to an upright. The slightest strain on the trip-wire would have caused the bombs to explode. This device was destroyed by the scouts.

RAIDS ON THE ENEMY LINES

At the end of January our D Company was lent to the 10th Brigade which was occupying the Chapelle Armentieres sector. This company along with D Company of the 44th Battalion formed part of a special Battalion called "X." Our D Company was away from us for five weeks, during which time the 10th Brigade had trained and carried out a raid. Raiding at this time had become a regular habit with Australians. The object of these raids was to examine the state of the enemy's front line and supports, and to find out what enemy units were opposed to us. This was called "Identification."

The raid carried out by the 42nd on February 1st, was like most of the raids carried out by other units, only partially successful. The raiding party consisted of three officers and 69 other ranks. In order to facilitate the approach to the point of assembly and to cross the snow covered ground of No-Man's Land, white suits were worn which proved invaluable by preventing detection on the journey in and out.

The 41st, 43rd, and 44th Battalions all conducted "raiding expeditions" on behalf of the 11th Brigade.

THE ENEMY RETURNS THE COMPLIMENT

With all this raiding activity on the part of the 11th Brigade it was not to be expected that the enemy would accept our attentions without attempting to reciprocate.

As we anticipated, his "return visit" eventuated in due course. The date of his "early morning call" on our Battalion was February the 14th. He signified his intention of "coming over" by dropping "visiting cards" in the shape of a barrage at 3.35 a.m. on our front line in the vicinity of Plank Avenue. An hour later the barrage ceased. It was then discovered his intended "surprise party" had arrived. They found us "At Home," and we gave them a "very warm reception," in fact we rather overdid the "welcome," for in less than two minutes "the party" was broken up, and the Hun was hunted home.

In the mix-up we sustained two casualties, but our rifle fire must have been effective for the body of a dead German was discovered next day in No-man's Land.

"SPIES"

During our occupation of L'Epinette and whilst billeted in Armentieres it was impressed upon all ranks to refrain from discussing anything of a military nature with strangers, or even among ourselves on account of the espionage known to be in existence. A great deal has been written on this subject, it is, however, significant and worth recording that not only were human beings regarded as spies, but ostensibly innocent birds and beasts became objects of suspicion.

The records of the 11th Brigade contain the information that on February the 5th, at noon, two pigeons flew over from Armentieres towards the enemy lines. The next day, a black dog endeavoured to get through one of the gaps in our defences. This animal was shot dead by a Lewis gunner. Again on February the 17th, more pigeons crossed our lines, and on that same night and on the night previous, lights were observed flashing from the enemy lines whilst at the same time a signalling light was noticed in the vicinity of Armentieres directed towards the enemy lines. This supplies a very obvious reason why raids in this sector were accompanied by so little success.

GAS

We continued our activities in the same manner until our relief on March 11th. Up to that time it has not been recorded that we were subjected to any gas attack, although the enemy was using it in the Sector we occupied. In fact, on February the 18th, gas shells were used on our sister Battalion, the 44th, from which happily no casualties resulted.

PONT DE NIEPPE AND PLOEGSTEERT

On March 12th, our C Company was lent to the 44th Battalion to take over a new system of trenches in Ploegsteert Wood. This place was generally spoken of as "Plugstreet." The reason of this loan was to allow the 44th to carry out the last raid of the 11th Brigade prior to its departure from L'Epinette.

On March 15th we left Armentieres and took over billets from the New Zealanders at Pont de Nieppe. We were immediately engaged on "working parties," and continued so until March 19th, when we took over the line in Ploegsteert Wood.

Here we became intimately acquainted with more varieties of enemy trench mortar bombs, which we christened Coal-boxes and Rum-jars. Then there were "pineapples" sometimes called "aerial torpedoes," a kind of rifle-grenade, so that the reception we got on arriving at Plugstreet was as varied as it was warm, especially as the Hun artillery introduced us to Whiz-Bangs, Pom-poms and other products of the "Krupp" family.

We heartily reciprocated those attentions by hurling to him Stokes Mortar bombs, and some of a far more aggressive and substantial kind, from a heavy trench mortar called "The Flying Pig."

The designations of various trenches in and around Ploegsteert Wood presented newcomers with the origin of the first occupants. For instance, it was easy to discern traces of London troops by the names of such localities and trenches as Hyde Park Corner, The Strand, Piccadilly, Regent Street, and St. James's, whilst the communicating trenches, Toronto and Ontario Avenues, indicated Canadians had been their occupants.

FURTHER ENEMY RAIDS

We were supported by New Zealanders on our left, and on March 23rd the enemy attacked the New Zealand Rifle Brigade and was repulsed. The bombardment just touched our left flank from which four casualties resulted.

We had suspicions that there was much likelihood of an enemy raid on our lines, and when on Saturday, March 24th, his artillery was particularly attentive to cutting our wire entanglements, and repeated the attentions on the following Monday, the 26th, our suspicions were confirmed.

On the night of the 26th, a heavy bombardment was laid on our lines. One minute later our S.O.S. signal was fired and this was immediately responded to by all batteries operating on S.O.S. lines. At three minutes past two, the first party of the enemy was observed in our wire.

A concentration of artillery was placed against the enemy lines. A party of raiders succeeded in reaching our parapet. We used bombs unsparingly, forcing them to withdraw without effecting an entry. In another place two of the enemy reached the top of the parapet. We wounded one of them, then both immediately made a hurried exit, leaving behind a bag of bombs and the cap of the wounded man.

At seven minutes past two a party of about twenty men was seen 40 yards away from our trenches, but no further attempt was made to enter our trenches after the withdrawal of the two isolated parties. The last of the retreating raiders was seen from our parapet at 2.25 a.m., and an hour later our patrol observed four of the enemy helping two of their wounded through the Bosche wire.

But we did not escape entirely unscathed. Our casualties were twelve wounded.

Prior to our occupation of this area it had been subject to raids by the enemy from which he had derived a certain amount of success. His failure on this occasion was attributed to the effective co-operation of all arms.

The fire of the Lewis guns and the Vickers guns in the region to be traversed in No-man's Land must have caused losses to the enemy whilst it is probable that fire from these guns prevented him from effecting an entry into our trenches.

We were not sorry when on the following day, March 27th, the 44th Battalion relieved us. We returned to Pont de Nieppe with the exception of No. 2 platoon, which was detached for work at Le Bizet.

On April the 4th, a week later, we relieved the 44th Battalion in Ploegsteert Wood. Employed mainly on repair and construction work and active patrolling, we continued there until April the 20th, when we were relieved by the 43rd Battalion.

OOSTHOVE FARM.

The scene of our recent operations was on the border of Flanders whilst our billets were at Pont de Nieppe, adjacent to the French frontier.

On being relieved at Ploegsteert (Belgium) we moved to billets on the Flemish border, where a large farm house called Oosthove Farm was occupied by us until towards the end of April. Here we experienced a slight relaxation from the arduous duties we had been called upon to perform daily, since our arrival in France. Nevertheless, we had to furnish our daily quota of working parties, and it always seemed to us that one's own particular platoon never escaped being called upon to perform whatever work was going.

OUR FIRST BIG ROUTE MARCH

The last days of April found us back again in Armentieres, where we remained for two days preparatory to removing to the Rest and Training Area in the district of St. Omer. It was at this time that we were afforded the opportunity of recording our votes for the Australian Commonwealth Elections, which to us seemed a remarkable thing, seeing that we were thousands of miles away from the land of our birth or adoption.

Up to this time, since our arrival in France each of the four Battalions comprising the 11th Brigade had been continuously in the front line trenches, either holding the line or engaged as working parties. After nearly four months it was decided to give us a spell in order to recuperate.

The weather had improved considerably. The winter

months had passed and May had opened up in all its traditional glory. We had the usual kit inspections and final inspections, and at length on May 1st, we set out on our four-day route march. We were informed that it was a competitive march, and that the four Battalions of the 11th Brigade were being watched to see whose performance was the best. Naturally we were all on our mettle, our Battalion motto being: "Cede Nullis" (yield to none).

In four days we performed a march of fifty and a-half miles, and this was the longest march we had ever undertaken. In spite of the long term we had served in the trenches and the rigorous winter we had experienced, it was apparent that we were still very fit, for on that long and exacting march only one man fell out from the column.

The first day we got as far as Pradelles (16½ miles), via Steenwerke and Merris. The second day we reached Renescure (13 miles), via Wallon Capelle, and Ebblinghem. The third day we got as far as Tatinghem (9 miles), via Arques and St. Omer, and at length on the fourth day we reached our destination, twelve miles distant. Each of our companies was billeted at different villages. They were named Alquines, Harlettes, and Fromentelle.

Tenacity

First Big Battle—Messines—Warneton

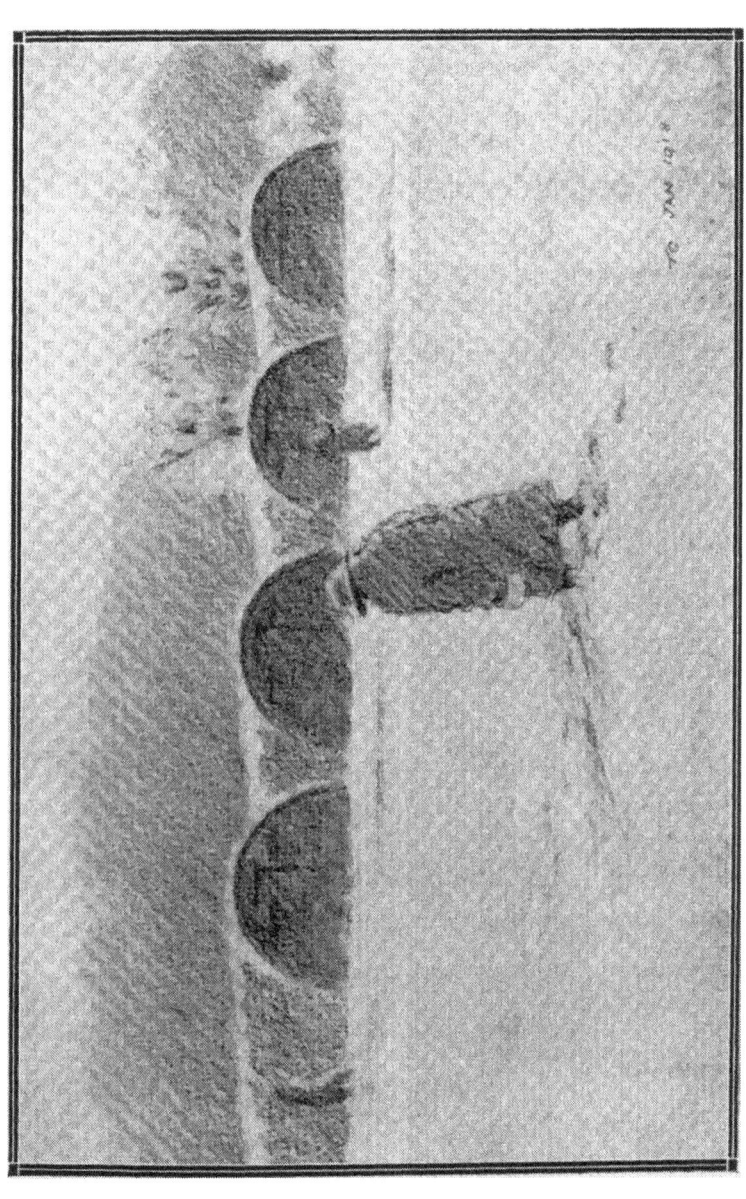

WATERLANDS CAMP (JESUS FARM). (Drawing by Tom Cross).

Keeping Fit

We were given one day's rest to recover from the fatigue of the march, but next day we started to train more intensively than ever. We had all the routine of bayonet fighting, physical jerks, and drill. Added to these we had to practice all sorts of new stunts and general attacking methods. This went on for three weeks, and that was what was called "a rest."

The relief from continuous shell and machine-gun fire, and the absence of the roar of the artillery was without doubt a rest to the mind and nerves, but of bodily rest there was no trace, if we except the one day's leave which was granted to all in order to visit the town of St. Omer.

Quite naturally we understood that something big was coming off soon, especially as we had to carry out practices over ground that we were told was similar to that over which we should have to operate.

On May 14th we were inspected by the General Officer Commanding the British Second Army Corps, and four days later the return march to the battle area began, May 18th.

We billeted for the night at Tatinghem, on the 19th Renescure was reached, on the 20th we overtook Strazelle, whilst the 21st found us back again in our old home-town of Armentieres.

PREPARATIONS FOR MESSINES BATTLE

On May 23rd, we proceeded to the trenches at Le Bizet where we relieved the 38th Battalion. Here we underwent ten days of heavy trench warfare, due to enemy bombardments which came over in reply to our excessive shelling. Preparatory to the Messines Battle, raids, bombing and gas attacks by both sides were frequent at all times, both day and night. The din and roar was incessant. There was not a moment's pause in the pounding of the artillery, heavy and light. The very air was full of activity, deadly and uncompromising. The enemy's display of lights of every kind was an imposing sight. On June 2nd we were relieved and billeted at Pont de Nieppe, where we remained until the night of June 6th. In the meantime, on June 5th, our Battalion carried out a successful raid in broad daylight. Among the enemy dead were found a large proportion of lads, apparently about 17 years old.

Whilst we were in Pont de Nieppe the enemy shelled the town so unmercifully that for two days and nights we were compelled to leave the town and take to the open fields. To add to our discomfort we had gas attacks to contend with.

On the morning of the 6th of June we attempted to have a parade, but when the enemy planted shells about fifty yards in front of us, the parade was abandoned. That night we fell in at 9 p.m. on our parade ground, which adjoined a cemetery. Here we remained until midnight, when heavily laden with bombs, flares, grenades, ammunition, rations, etcetera, we made our way up to the trenches by a circuitous and, to us, hitherto unknown route.

At this point both artilleries were quiet, but an hour or so after, both sides opened out with a fury that was terrific. The Germans supplemented their shells with gas, which later on, became so heavy that we had to adjust our gas masks as we stumbled along in the darkness to our position in Bunhill Row, Ploegsteert, which we eventually reached at 3.0 a.m.

Our strength at this time was 35 officers and 976 other ranks. We were scarcely in position before a huge mine on which British engineers and sappers had been working for many months was exploded. This took place at 3.10 a.m. on the morning of June 7th. The ground trembled and everything rocked. The sensation it caused among our own troops was awesome. The noise of the terrific explosion was heard as far away as England.

It destroyed the enemy's defence system and spread demoralisation among his troops. This of course, was the object for which the mine had been laid.

And thus began the first big battle in which our Battalion was employed.

OUR OBJECTIVE

The objective of the 3rd Australian Division was to attack and consolidate, firstly, the Black Line, and secondly the Green Line. The 9th and 10th Brigades attacked respectively on the right and left, whilst the 11th Brigade was held in reserve.

The area over which our engagement took place was divided into sectors, shown on the military maps by different coloured markings, so that our objectives were distinguished by calling them certain coloured lines.

The enemy's lines no longer existed. For many hundreds of yards nothing remained of all his elaborate defence system but junks of iron and splintered wood all mixed up with piles of heaved up brown earth.

Naturally, when prisoners first began to come in they were objects of much curiosity and interest, but when they were coming along in droves and we became more accustomed to the taking of German prisoners, so the interest in them declined. Both artilleries continued their heavy bombardments, that of the enemy caused much discomfiture to us by reason of it pouring in poison gas.

In the early morning of June 8th, we moved back for a brief respite to a place known as "The Catacombs. This was the name given to a huge dug-out built in the side of a hill, and so large that it was capable of accommodating a whole brigade of men.

THE BLACK LINE

At midnight on June 8th, we took over that particular area known to us as "The Black Line." It was our job to strongly consolidate it. For five days we remained here digging and strengthening the defences to withstand any counter attacks. Our position was so advanced that Messines, once a prosperous town, now only just a heap of ruins, was lying far away to the rear.

During this period we repulsed several counter-attacks and were subjected to intense bombardments as we dug ourselves in. Our casualties were, in consequence, both numerous and severe. The stench from the tremendous number of Germans lying unburied in front of us was nauseating.

At midnight on the 11th of June we were relieved and proceeded to Hillside Camp, Neuve Eglise, where we billeted for two days in tents. We moved out on the 14th, to the village of Doullieu, quite close to the town of Bailleul.

Our strength at this time was 826 officers and men. Prior to the Messines Battle it was 1011. Our losses in this operation were therefore 185 officers and men.

After a short spell we returned to Hillside Camp, Neuve Eglise. On June 22nd it was found that our strength had increased to 34 officers and 818 other ranks, due to the new draft which had arrived.

WE RETURN TO THE BLACK LINE

On June 23rd, we returned to the Black Line and the Green Line. Here we remained for a period of twenty-one days, during which we consolidated and strengthened our new line of defence.

The communicating trenches were named: Unbearable, Gapaard, Hun's Walk, Owl, Fanny, and Wellington. These were all in bad condition. The Front Line was not joined up. Water was two feet deep in some parts of the trenches owing to continuous wet weather.

There was a great scarcity of engineering material, but in spite of all these drawbacks we made good progress by steadily gaining ground and pushing out strong posts in the direction of Warneton.

Our casualties were not severe, but never a day passed without toll being taken of our comrades by death or wounds.

The enemy presented evidence of nervousness and anxiety. He became very active with patrols and succeeded in establishing several strong posts in No-man's Land, which it was our object to eliminate, resulting in the action known as

THE WARNETON STUNT

We were relieved in the Messines sector on July 11th by the 36th Battalion and moved into tents and shelters by the side of a small streamlet called "Le Petit Douve."

Thence onwards until the end of July a continuous series of downpours saturated the ground, turning it into one huge bog. The little streamlet became a swiftly flowing river, ready to burst its banks at any moment, so that the conditions under which we existed were most discomforting.

Our strength was increased on July 14th by a draft of 108, and again on the 16th by a further draft of 50.

The Warneton Stunt, which we carried out in conjunction with the 43rd Battalion, although directed mainly towards wiping out the enemy's strong posts established in No-man's Land, which had caused us so much annoyance, was also devised to serve as a diversion for the offiensive taking place on the North-west (Belgium) Front.

On the night of July 31st we returned to the trenches, performing part of the journey by motor lorries. The ground was so water logged that it took five hours to make the approach march.

The 43rd Battalion attacked on the right. The 42nd Battalion attacked on the left. The operation was highly successful. Strong post after strong post was attacked and captured along with many prisoners and counter-attacks beaten off. It is estimated that 150 of the enemy were killed in our first attack.

Our casualties were fairly light but our captures were many. Our men were utterly exhausted by the strain of fifty hours continuous fighting and digging, in the most abominable weather. The Corps Commander awarded eight of our men military medals for their conspicuous achievements on this occasion.

JESUS FARM

On August 4th, we moved back to Waterlands Camp near Steenwerke. This camp was more generally known as Jesus Farm, probably so named from the Crucifix which stood at the roadside. Shrines and crucifixes abounded in all villages in this vicinity, and were found at almost every cross road. Here, at Jesus Farm, we found good wooden huts which were greatly appreciated after our long spell in the open.

Owing to many of our observation balloons flying high in the sky above this location, our camp received a great deal of shrapnel intended for the Balloons. We were frequently spectators of thrilling escapes by the observers when the balloons they occupied were set on fire.

DESTRUCTION OF BALLOONS

The enemy utilised diverse means to destroy our balloons. Sometimes they were shelled intermittently with shrapnel which exploded in the air, and sometimes he would send over small aeroplanes fitted with machine-guns which fired incendiary bullets. These small planes usually hid behind a cloud. Seizing a favourable opportunity, they would dart quickly across to our lines, fire the balloon and flit rapidly back again.

So swiftly was the act performed that before one had time to realise what was happening, the balloon, sometimes two and three, in rapid succession, vanished before our eyes in clouds of smoke and flame.

Hostile aircraft hovered daily over our heads, and on several occasions we became excited witnesses of enemy planes being caught in the glare of our searchlightts, whilst anti-aircraft guns, called "Archies," peppered away harmlessly at the sky. Being quite close to Steenwerke, we were frequent visitors to that town, which abounded in canteens, egg and chip joints, and estaminets. An object of particular interest to us was the Stone Grotto and Altar, cut out of the wall of solid rock in the main street.

REMILLY—WERQUIN.

Our tenancy of Jesus Farm expired on August 22nd, when we entrained at Bailleul for Wizernes, whence we marched to the village of Remilly—Werquin, where we billeted in barns. We had quite a pleasant stay there until September 26th. Apparently, we were the first Australians to be billeted in this district and the villagers did not understand our peculiarities. However, on better acquaintance, they warmed up to us and we became very good friends.

It was here that we came across some strange troops belonging to the army of one of our allies, the Portuguese. They were resting in villages adjacent to ours, but we could not form strong attachments with them, on the contrary, many a "scrap" took place between us. We always referred to them as "Pork and Beans," or "Pork and Cheese."

The towns of Lumbres and St. Omer, being quite near, our visits there were frequent.

Although the weather was very pleasant and we were supposed to be resting, heavy training was the order of the day in anticipation of the offensive which it was known would soon be launched in the Ypres sector.

Endurance

Third Battle of Ypres—Broodseinde—Passchendaele

THIRD BATTLE OF YPRES.
Australian Wounded awaiting transport to the Casualty Clearing Station.

Poperinghe

Our rest came to end on September 25th, when we set out on our march to Blairingham. We proceeded next day to Eeke, and continued our march to Poperinghe, which place we eventually reached on September 27th. This last day was very trying, for the weather was hot and very dusty. It was a bad day for marching, so that we were very glad when we at last made our camp, near the Railway Depot, one mile east of the town. Unfortunately, our rest was broken through the enemy bombing us, which resulted in casualties to men and horses.

Next day, the 28th, we were again bombed, and again, on the 29th, hostile aircraft dropped bombs throughout the night, which inflicted heavy casualties, especially on the 11th Brigade Machine Gun Company, among whom were many former 42nd Battalion men.

Our strength at the end of September was 43 officers, 978 other ranks. We were bombed again on October 1st, causing us further casualties. On October 2nd, we entrained at Poperinghe for Ypres. Reaching there, we bivouacked at a location near a cemetery a little after midday.

THIRD BATTLE OF YPRES.
BROODSEINDE

At 10 p.m. on the night of October 3rd the approach march began. We found marching a very difficult performance owing to the several sharp showers which had rendered the ground sodden and sticky and made visibility very poor. Fortunately the route was marked by tapes, white posts, and red lights, and these were more or less discernable in the dark.

The assembly point (that is, the place where those

about to engage in the offensive had to congregate), was near Zonnebeke Railway Station. The time for the hop-over was drawing near. At 5.15 a.m. the first definite information of the nearness of zero hour was given by our artillery putting down a heavy barrage, which moved forward about 300 yards.

Naturally, the enemy retaliated with heavy artillery fire which caused many losses among the men who were in the rear sections. These sections of the rear were hastily brought forward from the danger zone and moved up Hill 40.

This meant that the entire Brigade was in massed formation, all troops having been crowded into a depth of at the most 100 yards. Emergency knows no law, and though at that time anything in the nature of a mass was almost suicidal, it had to be done. During the assembly one or two bridges over the Zonnebeke were smashed. All troops had to cross over one bridge, and this was responsible for some little delay and a few casualties.

An examination of the ground between Zonnebeke and the Front Line proved how difficult was the assembly of the 11th Brigade, and for the satisfactory manner in which it took place, credit was given to the 11th Field Company Engineers for the laying of the tapes and to the Pioneers for the marking of tracks.

At last the great moment came. Punctually at 6 a.m. our artillery came down on the enemy lines with ferocity and accuracy. Our barrage fell like a wall of flame. Simultaneously, the whole Brigade rose as one man and went forward to the attack.

Enemy troops in the front line offered stout resistance for several minutes, but our advancing troops were not to be denied. A great number of enemy dead were found shortly after, making it evident this line had been very heavily held. The 43rd Battalion reached its objective without difficulty. The 42nd advanced behind the 43rd. Two officers were killed and one officer wounded before Hill 40 was crossed.

The first objective was reached at 6.20 a.m. and consolidation was commenced immediately.

At forty-one minutes after zero hour, the 42nd Battalion leap-frogged through the 43rd, and continued the attack.

Owing to the swampy ground and heavy travelling, the company of the Battalion operating on our left failed to keep up with the barrage, and this drew our left company about 500 yards over to the left. This was remedied by the Commander of our A Company, which was in reserve, who acted promptly and threw his men into the gap. Then all went well and our left company resumed its position.

The enemy kept firing Verey light signals as our troops advanced, and his artillery kept shortening the range. Thames Wood was shelled heavily, and that was where, at this stage, most of our casualties were sustained.

During the advance from first to second objective (the red line), large numbers of enemy troops were observed running towards our advancing troops. As their positions were not known, they were fired on, causing casualties, but when it was found that they wished to surrender, they were allowed to drift through our troops. Escorts were provided at the rate of one man to twenty prisoners.

Our objective was reached on time and consolidation at once started. The barrage halted 200 yards beyond the Red Line for forty-seven minutes. Large numbers of prisoners were coming in, altogether one hundred of them were taken by the 42nd alone, in this area.

A dugout used by the enemy as an aid post was captured by us together with the whole medical staff. This dugout also contained a machine-gun. Nine enemy machine-guns were captured by us, four of which were entirely new, having never been used.

The ground was very wet and shell-torn, which rendered the work of consolidation very arduous, but in two hours our men were well under cover.

The work of evacuating the wounded was rendered extremely difficult due to the long and heavy carry and intense enemy barrages.

During the afternoon of October 4th the enemy made repeated counter attacks on our front which was then held by the 41st Battalion. These were all repulsed. He made further counter-attacks the following day, and was again beaten off.

On the morning of October 6th, we were relieved, after having been in the line continuously for sixty hours. Our casualties were: Officers, 4 killed, 7 wounded; other ranks, 220 killed and wounded.

On Sunday, October 7th, we rested at St. Lawrence Camp, Brandhoek. The roads and ground were in a deplorable condition. Our strength was 32 officers, 773 other ranks.

THIRD BATTLE OF YPRES.

PASSCHENDAELE

On October 8th, we started preparations for another move to the Ypres front, to take over from the 66th (British) Division. On October 9th a party of our men consisting of 16 officers and 400 other ranks moved via Ypres and encamped in tents on the eastern slopes of the Friezenberg Ridge. This party was called "A" Eschelon.

Another section called "B" Eschelon, consisting of 12 officers and 240 other ranks (transport and Quartermaster's personnel), proceeded from Brandhoek and camped in tents east of Ypres, whilst two officers and 80 other ranks were despatched for duty with the 11th Brigade Engineers.

The weather was bad and the ground boggy, which rendered transport very difficult. Heavy rain fell at intervals throughout the day and night.

The 66th (British) Division attacked on October 11th, but the result was only a partial success, owing to the abnormal weather, the exhausted condition of the men, and the awful state of the ground. On the night of 10/11th the 11th Brigade relieved British troops and the 42nd and 44th Battalions held the front line. The 41st and 43rd Battalions were in reserve, 400 yards in rear. Our Battalion took over from an exhausted British regiment which had suffered severely. They occupied the left front from Ravenbeke to Augustus Wood.

The men whom we relieved had suffered so badly that we found many of them in a state of complete exhaustion, which rendered them targets for enemy snipers. In one small section alone. fifty-seven of them had been sniped in one day. Their dead and dying lay around in heaps, whilst their numerous wounded were groaning and unattended. Those who formed the survivors had very little food.

The relief had to be carried out in daylight and the enemy observed the movement. His artillery immediately put down a barrage which inflicted many casualties upon us and disorganised the relief. Prior to our taking over the line, no attempt at consolidation had been attempted, so we had to occupy shell holes and carry out the work of consolidation as well as circumstances would permit. The weather was atrocious. The ground was so saturated that every trench as it was dug immediately filled with water, and had to be abandoned for a fresh position.

During the first twelve hours of our occupation of this position enemy snipers were very active. Mention is made in Brigade records of the wonderful activity of our patrols, one party on the left, penetrating as far as 1000 yards towards Passchendaele without getting in touch with the enemy. The 9th and 10th Brigades attacked on the morning of October 13th. The 11th Brigade became Divisional Reserve. The 42nd Battalion occupied shell holes.

At this stage no less than thirty-three per cent. of our men had to be evacuated. As the men of the "A" Eschelon were gradually sent back to the transport lines their places were taken by men of the "B" Eschelon. These were cooks, brakesmen, batmen, bandsmen, and other Quarter-master's details. Foot trouble was the main cause of the disablement of our men, combined with the effects of mustard gas.

The damage by this kind of gas was caused through men sitting or lying on ground upon which gas shells had burst. The parts of the body which came in contact with the ground became blistered and very painful.

The attack of the 9th and 10th Brigades resulted in the 9th reaching its objective, whilst the 10th was held up West of Passchendaele.

On the night of October 13th, the 9th and 10th Brigade troops were withdrawn and the 11th Brigade once more held the line. Most of our men were by this time completely done up. Many dropped down by the wayside as they doggedly toiled along to their assigned positions. When they got there, the line was found to be, instead of advanced, some thirty yards behind where we had originally left it. The ground was all shell stricken and sodden.

Some of the wounded Tommies were there yet. They were in an appalling state. Our fellows gave them all their food and water, but were obliged to get on with the job that was before them. Our casualties were again numerous, so we availed ourselves of the shelter of shell holes and abandoned "pill-boxes," which gave some protection from the incessant shelling.

The shell holes were half full of water and the "pill-boxes" contained a full complement of dead and dying of both sides.

"Pill-box" was the name given to that particular form of concrete dugout which the enemy constructed in the form of an enlarged box, of the type in which Beechams Pills are usually contained.

In one of the "pill-boxes" no less than twenty-four wounded men were assembled, all of whom were eventually evacuated. Others, however, were not so fortunate, for regrettable as it may be, it has to be admitted that many of our own, as well as the enemy's wounded, found graves in that awful sea of mud.

The stench from the dead was fearful. They were lying in all directions in various stages of decomposition.

The 42nd Battalion was left support behind the 41st Battalion, occupying positions in the vicinity of Abraham's Heights. Here the troops had to hold on for forty-eight hours. No offensive action could be taken on account of the exhausted condition of the men and the state of the weather.

On the night of October 16th, we were relieved and remained in reserve until the night of October 21st, when Canadians took over from us and we moved to a camp west of Ypres.

OUR DEPLETED RANKS

The total of the casualties that occurred during the period October 4th to October 21st, was 438. We had five officers killed and ten wounded. Other ranks suffered to the extent of 62 killed and 361 wounded, sick and missing. Our fighting strength was reduced to but 11 officers and 180 other ranks.

During this period both men and animals suffered severely, and the resources of the Battalion were strained to the utmost. The difficulties of transport were enormous. All material and rations had to be carried by pack mules along bog-like tracks and over shell torn ground, whilst added to these tremendous handicaps was the ceaseless attention of the enemy, who shelled our approaches continuously. Yet despite all these obstacles, rations, water, dry socks and ammunition were taken up daily, and after the first two days, hot tea and soup were conveyed to us in improvised containers, such as kerosene tins which were wrapped in blankets.

The work of the Battalion's transport was outstanding throughout these operations. The men showed the utmost grit and kept the Battalion going under the worst conditions imaginable.

Never since its formation had the men of the Battalion faced such abnormal weather, never had men been called upon to face greater hardships, or to display greater fortitude, and endurance, and it may safely be recorded that never have troops, officers and men alike responded more splendidly to such inexorable demands.

RE-ORGANISATION

Quite naturally, it was impossible for any unit to continue its work with such depleted strength, and it was welcome news to the tired and exhausted remnant of our indomitable Battalion when the word was given round: "We're going back to Remilly-Werquin to re-organise."

Accordingly, "all that was left of us" moved back on October 22nd. Some travelled by motor buses and the rest by railway train from Ypres to Wizernes, marching thence to Remilly-Werquin where the same billets were occupied as before.

The weather this time was not so pleasant. We experienced many miserable days, accompanied by frost and much rain. A good deal of sickness broke out in the way of colds, influenza, and chest troubles. And this was scarcely to be wondered at, seeing the ordeal the men had recently undergone.

Continuous training, with frequent route marches

gradually brought fitness to the ranks and continued to do so until November 12th, when we set out again for the forward area. Fine weather prevailed and the troops marched 12½ miles the first day, performing the job in good style.

We billeted in farm-houses at Bolseghem. Next day we did an 18½ mile march to Le Becque, near Steenwerke, during which much endurance was exhibited. The Battalion came right through without a man falling out. On November 15th, we marched another seven miles, which brought us to

KORTEPYP

This name was derived from the estaminet in the locality called in French Corte-Pipe, in English, short pipe, and in Flemish it is Korte-Pyp.

Here we billeted in wooden huts and did some intense training daily. Every morning three and a-half hours were devoted to routine military drill and exercise, whilst every afternoon two hours were given to recreational training. Football was the main sport. Inter-platoon and inter-company matches were organised.

It was at this time that the 42nd football war cry was first heard. Although consisting of nothing more formidable than harmless words such as potato, tomato, banana, plum, tobacco, and a boast intimating that the 42nd Battalion was always on top, it sounded very menacing and defiant when yelled by our side to the rival team. Matches between units of the 11th Brigade and the Artillery took place every Wednesday and Saturday afternoon. These sports gatherings were sometimes disorganised by enemy airmen who came over in planes called "Gothas." The unmistakable drone of the Gothas which announced their arrival was the signal for both teams, as well as spectators, to hastily scatter.

The 11th Brigade was now in reserve. The strength of the Battalion was, on December 1st, 40 officers and 742 other ranks. The health of the Battalion steadily improved. The weather though intensely cold was nice and dry.

Adjacent to the camp was a large marquee, erected by the Y.M.C.A., and a very excellent canteen was also established.

ON THE MOVE AGAIN

We remained at Kortepyp until the middle of the month, when we set out for Waterlands Camp, billeting at Locre en route. On the 19th December we set out for the "old habitation" which we called Jesus Farm, and found it to be what we termed "a very cold joint," owing to the scarcity of fuel which prevailed at that time. Everything of a burnable nature was utilised by us in order to keep our fires and braziers going.

BOIS GRENIER

On the night of December 20th, we took over the Bois Grenier sector. Our Battalion occupied a full brigade front. The front line was held lightly by a system of infantry posts closely supported by Lewis gun posts which covered the gaps. The trenches were in good condition and damaged very little by shell fire. We found it a very quiet sector with good shelters and splendid facilities for getting hot food to the front line.

During our six days in this sector the temperature was below zero. We were fortunate in having no cases of trench feet despite the fact that the ground was white with snow and frost.

CHRISTMAS 1917

We spent the festive season in the trenches, under much the same conditions as last year, only on this occasion we were experienced and seasoned soldiers.

On Christmas Eve we heard the Fritzes singing away, but though the enemy appeared to have developed the "Goodwill to all Men" spirit, we made no attempt to reciprocate or fraternise.

To spite us for this, he next day savagely and severely shelled Bois Grenier and the adjacent town of Erquinhem, causing considerable damage, happily only to the roads.

On December 27th, we handed over to the 43rd Battalion and returned to Jesus Farm. The weather was severely cold. Frost rendered the roads so slippery that marching was a difficult operation.

CHRISTMAS DINNER

Owing to our occupancy of the front line on Christmas Day, it was not possible for us to hold our Christmas dinner on December 25th. We were, however, not to be denied an event like that for the sake of a mere date. We held our Christmas dinner on December 30th, and a real good dinner it was, while it lasted, which was not very long. That very same night we were employed on working parties in the Bois Grenier and Armentieres sectors. Six of our men received their medals on this day at the hands of our Corps Commander, General Sir William Birdwood.

On the last day of 1917 we marched away from Jesus Farm. The roads were like glass and the weather piercingly cold.

When at last we reached our destination at Locre, much difficulty was experienced in obtaining fuel for even cooking purposes, owing to the short issue.

NEW YEAR'S DAY 1918

New Year's Day found us at Birr Barracks, adjacent to Locre, a clean little village on the Belgian frontier. Here we received further reinforcements which brought up our strength to 26 officers and 1063 other ranks.

Drill competitions showed a marked improvement in training. January 27th found us on the move from Locre to Kortepyp, whence we next day shifted to Ingersoll Camp, Nieppe.

INGERSOLL CAMP

This was an encampment of wooden huts near to the town of Nieppe on the road to Romarin. Whilst here we were engaged on working parties, going out both day and night to the Le Bizet and Ploegsteert sectors.

To get to the trenches we used a light railway which the enemy had ranged to a nicety. Many a lucky escape was experienced on the journeys to and fro. On more than one occasion we had to hurriedly leave our train and continue the journey as pedestrians instead of passengers.

Whilst at Ingersoll Camp we heard persistent rumours that a German offensive was expected with the arrival of spring, and that it was thought the attempt to break through would be on the Armentieres—Messines Front. Our labours to fortify and strengthen our defences became ceaseless and strenuous.

A SCENE ON THE MENIN ROAD.

CONCERT PARTIES

Two Australian military concert parties entertained us in Nieppe. One was supplied by the 44th Battalion, and the other, a much more pretentious organisation, was provided by Divisional Headquarters. This latter party was recruited from every unit of the Third Division, and gave us some first-class shows. The singing, acting, choral work, and comedy, was of a high order, whilst an orchestra of twenty talented musicians provided us with many a musical treat. The "girl" of the company, who of course was an Australian soldier, was one of the leading features.

These military concert parties were greatly appreciated by us for they did much to keep our spirits high and helped us to forget, for the time being, the hardship, death and destruction surrounding us.

FEBRUARY 1918

We went back to the trenches on February 5th, this time at Pont Rouge, where we remained for a period of eight days. When we came out of the line, we played several football matches, having at one time for our opponents the Royal West Kent Regiment. We again spent much of our time making defence works, and many new dugouts of reinforced concrete were constructed within old buildings.

Enemy aircraft were very active, but our airmen having dominance kept hostile planes well away from our lines.

On February 21st, some of our planes went for an excursion over the German lines, leaving souvenirs of their visit in the form of bombs. The enemy provided a magnificent display of fireworks in order to direct his anti-aircraft guns.

On this date we returned to the trenches at Pont Rouge, and remained there until March 2nd. Our term in the line on this occasion was particularly quiet, our main activities being confined to intensive patrolling.

BACK TO THE REST AREA

And now began preparatons for the long-promised, well-merited, and much-needed "rest."

On March 4th the Battalion set out from Ingersoll Camp for Kortepyp. The following day, the transport started on its journey to the "rest area," and on March 6th, the 42nd Battalion marched out of Kortepyp Camp at 11.30 in the morning, reaching Steenwerke at 1 o'clock. In less than three hours we had entrained and were well on the way to Lottinghem, which village was reached at 11.30 that night.

The Y.M.C.A. was already established there and supplied us with hot coffee. We partook of a hurried meal, then off we marched in the highest spirits on the seven-mile journey that was to bring us to our respective billets, namely, Harlettes for A and C Companies and Bulescamps for B Company. D Company and Headquarters were billeted at Fromenthal. It was not until 2.30 in the morning that we settled down to sleep. The transport arrived a few hours later.

When we woke up we realised that we were far from the roar of the guns. Free from the anxiety of raids with strict military discipline somewhat relaxed. We were filled with joyful anticipation of four weeks' serenity and relaxation.

But alas! Our month's holiday consisted of but thirteen days. The usual training was continued daily right up to March 20th, when our "visit to the country" came to abrupt termination.

THE STORM BREAKS

On March 21st the Battalion received warning to be prepared to move off at six hours' notice.

As some sort of solace to our feelings of disappointment we were paid that afternoon. Next day, the expected happened. Orders arrived at 4 a.m. for the Battalion to move immediately to Steenvorde. The transport got on its way at 10 a.m., and was followed half an hour later by Headquarters and D Company from Fromenthal. The other three companies were picked up at Bulescamps. Lottinghem was reached at 1 o'clock p.m. Two hours after, we were entrained and on our way to Ecke. We arrived there at 11 o'clock that night, detrained and marched to Steenvorde, and by midnight were all billeted.

The next day, March 23rd, all surplus equipment and extra blankets were discarded and dumped. The 42nd Battalion, all ready and prepared, awaited the issue of further commands.

So this was the "end of a perfect holiday." As events turned out there was to be no more rest for the 42nd, nor any other Australian unit until the cessation of hostilities.

Determination

**Off to the Somme—Stemming the Enemy Onrush—
Battle of Hamel**

The German Onslaught

On March 21st, the Germans attacked the front of the Fifth British Army in the Somme region. The tremendous number of enemy troops released from the Eastern Front by the collapse of the Russian forces, enabled him to launch an attack so fierce and powerful as to crumple up the forces opposing him on this part of the Somme Front selected by him for his attack.

It was also apparent that an attack on the Flanders Front was contemplated by our foes.

The Third Division was therefore moved in readiness to repel any attack on the Flanders Front, but suddenly this plan was altered. The movement of our Battalion was arrested on March 24th. The position on the Somme had become desperate. We received orders to immediately proceed southwards.

Accordingly at 8 o'clock on the morning of March 24th, we retraced our footsteps, arriving at Ecke at 10 a.m. Here we found motor buses in readiness to transport us. We got away at 11.30 a.m. and travelled via Capelle, Cassell to Ebblinghem, where we alighted and marched to Lynde. Here our transport joined us. We were all billeted by 4 in the afternoon.

ARQUES

The next day, March 25th, we proceeded to Arques, a distance of seven miles. It was a strenuous march through the rain and considered a remarkably good performance. Arriving in the early hours of the morning, a scene of great animation and activity presented itself to our eyes. The town teemed with troops belonging to every unit of the 11th Brigade. Trains were running hours behind schedule. Bicycles and gear were to be seen hanging between trucks and in a few instances, on top of them. We ate our meals in the streets and slept on the roadside, feeling thankful for the slightest shelter that was available.

OFF TO THE SOMME

At length, at 8 o'clock on March 26th, we entrained, leaving one hour later for Doullens, which town was reached at 3 in the afternoon. Anxiously awaiting the arrival of troops were Marshal Foch and Field Marshal Sir Douglas Haig, who had been attending that historic and momentous conference at which Marshal Foch was appointed to the supreme command of the Allied Armies.

After detraining, little time was lost. We marched off gaily singing "It's a Long Way to Tipperary," amidst wild cheers of congested throngs of French refugees. Pressing on, we reached a place called Thievres at midnight. Here we had a brief spell and partook of a drink of hot tea. We were unable to occupy the billets that had been allotted to us for the simple reason that the territory was apparently in the hands of the enemy.

THE RETREAT OF THE FIFTH ARMY

The scene that unfolded itself was one of the utmost confusion. We saw retreating troops of the Fifth Army intermingled with hundreds of French civilian refugees, thronging the highway and seriously impeding our forward movement. To make matters worse, a rumour got into circulation that German armoured cars were approaching, and that they were only three miles away. Those supposed armoured cars turned out to be merely a collection of agricultural machines which a noisy tractor was doing its best to save.

A more pitiable sight could not be imagined than the plight of those unfortunate refugees who had evacuated their beautiful homes and flourishing farms, or had abandoned their businesses and property to the tender mercy of whomsoever chanced to come along.

There were old men, women, and children, wheeling barrows on which had been hastily thrown the only possessions they were able to save. There were aged couples, in carts piled with bedding and household chattels, behind which was tethered a cow or perhaps two or more. Others just carried a small bundle containing but a few clothes and a little food.

Hopelessly mixed up with all this movement towards the rear, was a steady stream of guns of all types and calibres, farm waggons, threshing machines, lorries, and service waggons.

The French refugees, whose eyes during the past few days had become used to gazing with hopeless despair upon retreating troops, were spellbound at the contrasting sight of Australian troops in full fighting kit, swinging along, joking, smoking and laughing, with bands playing, marching in perfect order, forward and onward to meet the advancing enemy.

Inspired with new hope, these poor souls stopped their retreat as they frantically cheered us and waved us on with cries of "Vive les Australiens."

We remained but one hour in Thievres, and then marched on for another mile and a-half when we were met by omnibuses which took us on to Franvilliers, situated on the main road to Amiens, arriving at 5 a.m. on March 27th. Here we alighted and marched on to Heilly, and were met by the Brigadier. Orders were immediately received to take up a defensive line between Mericourt and Sailly le Sec with the River Somme on our right flank.

THE DIVISIONAL COMMANDER'S COMMENTS

Our Divisional Commander, General Sir John Monash, was at Franvilliers in a state of intense suspense and expectancy.

"My anxiety was relieved," Sir John Monash has written, "when a convoy of thirty buses arrived crowded with the staunch, reliable troops of the 11th Infantry Brigade.

"The spectacle of that Infantry," he continues, "will be ever memorable to me as one of the most inspiring sights of the whole war. Here was the Third Division—the 'New Chum' Division—which in spite of its great successes in Belgium and Flanders had never been able to boast like its sister Divisions that it had been 'down on the Somme'—come into its own at last, and called upon to prove its mettle.

"No one who saw those Battalions, in spite of the fatigue of two sleepless nights, marching on that clear crisp spring morning, with head erect and the swing and precision of a Royal Review Parade, could doubt that not a man of them would flinch from any assault that was likely to fall on them, nor was there a man who did not fully grasp that upon him and his companions was about to fall the **whole responsibility of frustrating the German attack to capture Amiens and separate the Allied Armies.**"

SAILLY LE SEC

At Heilly we dumped our packs and assumed "fighting order." The companies marched out in platoons at intervals and advanced to their respective positions. Although we had not known a hot meal for forty-eight hours and did not know when we were likely to get one, our spirits were of the best. Some of the men, being good scouts, looked around and discovered good food awaiting them. The inhabitants of the village having fled hurriedly, the meals they had spread and intended to eat, had been left upon the tables undisturbed, and so it happened, many an aching void that had taken possession of a 42nd stomach was relieved by this timely, welcome, and unexpected turn of Providence.

The River Ancre was crossed, and at about noon the village of Sailly le Sec was reached. Here we dug ourselves in. What little defence existed at the time of our arrival was furnished by remnants of the 9th Highland Regiment and cavalry outposts of the Queen's Bays.

The front held by the 42nd Battalion was roughly 2,000 yards. The cavalry in action could be discerned on the ridge between the rivers Ancre and Somme. They worked wonders in keeping the enemy at bay and by gaining information by patrolling.

An old-time system, made by the French at the beginning of the War, was converted into trenches, which were fairly good although dugouts were somewhat crude. The materials for making them we obtained from houses in the deserted village. A sheet of iron from one, a door from another. From others floorboards, straw, cushions, and even bedding. These all went to make our trench residences more homelike.

Our fighting in Northern France and Flanders had been associated mainly with mud and at the best, uninteresting tunnels, saps and labyrinths of trenches. But here was a contrast. We could not help comparing, unconsciously perhaps, our previous experiences with this countryside of such marvellous beauty. The scenes over which our operations were now taking place consisted of green fields, wheat crops, and prolific cultivation. Sheep and cattle, abandoned by their owners in their hurried exodus, browsed unconcernedly before our trenches.

Here we found no shell-holes, nor craters to disturb and despoil the contour of the landscape. Free from shrieking shells and the ceaseless rattle of machine-guns, the place possessed an aspect of serenity and peace rather than that of the crash and din of battle.

The village of Sailly le Sec on being explored was found to contain some very fine houses, well kept, and excellently furnished. In most of them paintings, statuary, and family treasures abounded. The Mairie, or residence of the Mayor, stood out conspicuously. In this was installed a piano of splendid appearance.

But it was in the cellars that our men discovered treasures more to their taste. Never had they seen such an abundance of wine. More plentiful than water. In fact there was no water in the water bottles whilst supplies of wine hung out, and every available vessel capable of holding liquid was utilised for carrying away the luscious beverage.

With poultry, eggs, sheep, pigs, and wine all to be had for the taking, the men of the 42nd had the time of their lives—but joy, at any time, is but fleeting—and particularly was it so in this instance. Before we had time to realise it, we were back at our job of fighting, and Sailly le Sec gradually became reduced to ruins.

SHRAPNEL GULLY

Next day, March 28th, we consolidated our position, and whilst doing so, carried out diligent and intensive patrolling.

One of our patrols encountered a German patrol of five, of whom they killed four and wounded one, who was brought in. This was the first of the numerous prisoners captured by us in the newly-established line. Two more prisoners were brought in later on in the evening. We sniped a considerable number of the enemy before the Front Line occupied by B Company. During the night the enemy was quiet, but we received information in a message dropped by one of our aeroplanes that the enemy was massing for an attack.

With the exception of four eighteen pounder guns of the Royal Horse Artillery, which had to cover the front of the entire Brigade, our operations up to this time had been unsupported by artillery. It was, therefore, a great relief to us to learn that our Third Divisional Artillery was gradually coming up and getting into action immediately upon arrival.

Our field cookers resumed business operations on March 29th. We were thus enabled to partake of hot meals once again.

The enemy's artillery resources were evidently accumulating, for on March 30th he became very active. Starting with a bombardment of Hamel on our right flank, at 10.30 a.m., using gas shells and high explosive, he next opened up on Bouzancourt, raining shells of all calibres upon that village.

THE GERMANS ATTACK OUR NEW LINE

At noon, our Front Line was subjected to severe shelling. It was quite obvious that a massed attack was imminent. After a few minutes hesitation the enemy began to advance.

Waves of enemy troops came steadily forward from Sailly Laurette on the south to the Corbie-Bray Road on the north, but all his assaults were frustrated. By midday the first phase of the attack, which was launched against our entire Front Line, had been held up by our machine-gun, Lewis-gun and rifle fire, and very shortly our defence was strengthened by the arrival of the Third Divisional Artillery, which immediately upon receiving word of the German attack, galloped gallantly into action, unlimbered the guns and poured devastating volleys into the advancing masses of troops.

The enemy gained about 400 yards of territory, which was not to his advantage for it brought his troops within range of our Infantry weapons.

At 2.15 p.m. another general advance on the whole Front was attempted. Re-inforcements were hurried by the enemy across the ridges. He attempted to advance his entire line, but so intense was the concentration of fire brought to bear upon the assaulting troops that the attack was completely repulsed.

In spite of heavy shelling and the immense number of troops hurled against us, the morale of the 42nd was never at a higher pitch. Men were actually laying wagers in francs as to which of them would be the first to hit a specified German.

Soon after 3 o'clock the enemy evidently realised the hopelessness of making any further progress. He began to dig-in for cover, in isolated positions, but when sunset arrived his intention to evacuate became obvious. Small parties of troops were seen dribbling away to the rear. His concentration of troops was gradually withdrawn. Due to the dull visibility which existed when the sun went down it was not possible to observe all the enemy's movements, but the continual progress of his troops from front to rear appeared to signify that he had no intention of holding the position in force. This conclusion on our part was verified during the night, when our patrols discovered that, with the exception of south of Sailly Laurette, the enemy had established a new Line.

It is estimated that at least a full Brigade of enemy troops attacked on the front occupied by the 42nd Battalion, and no less than 500 casualties were inflicted on the attackers. His wounded were heard moaning throughout the night, and were to be seen in considerable numbers when daylight broke.

Thus were broken up two very definite attacks on a large scale. Every attempt of smaller units to rush forward was utterly frustrated.

Throughout the attack our men were well supplied with ammunition. As a result of their victory, they appreciated more than ever the value of the rifle and the conservation of ammunition.

ENEMY MACHINE GUNNERS

With his most advanced troops, the enemy had invariably light machine-guns. These were worked in groups of four. The crews could be seen distinctly in the advance, also when setting up a position. In consequence, they were subjected to a great deal of fire, yet they worked fearlessly in a most aggressive manner. They were responsible for at least 50 per cent. of our casualties. Our stretcher-bearers, runners, signallers, carrying-parties, and so forth, suffered severely from this cause. During the enemy's withdrawal, these machine-gunners were, if anything, more savage than during the attack. They were the last troops to be withdrawn, with the exception of the snipers.

OUR WORK APPRECIATED BY THE GENERAL STAFF

Our runners, signallers, and liaison patrols kept the Battalion well supplied with all necessary and vital information.

All ranks received high commendation for the splendid work performed on this occasion, special mention was made of the reconnaisance work of the Adjutant, and of the capable observation maintained by the Intelligence Officer during the battle.

Ten other ranks received special mention and were recommended for various distinctions and awards, which were in due course conferred. There was, however, one instance of an N.C.O., who, at a time when so large a number of heroic acts and brave deeds were being performed, was particularly singled out and recommended for the Distinguished Conduct Medal. His bravery was conspicuous, and yet he did not receive the coveted award for he did not survive the serious wounds he received, and the distinction, not being posthumous, could not be awarded. The facts relative to the recommendation may well be recorded here, in order to exemplify that bravery, heroism, comradeship, and devotion to duty from which sprang "The Spirit of the Forty-second."

"On the evening of March 28, this sergeant was sent out with two sections to establish two observation posts in the face of the enemy.

When leaving our Line, the party was observed by the enemy and heavily shelled. The sergeant was stunned by a shell which exploded within a few feet of him. On regaining consciousness, he led the party

(Drawing by Tom Cross).

WATER-MILL AT REMILLY—WERQUIN.
A Village where the Battalion Rested on two occasions.

out and successfully established his posts, and in course of so doing, came under heavy fire from two machine-guns.

"Later in the evening, the post was rushed by an enemy party of seven. Allowing them to approach to within bombing distance, he ordered his men to 'fire,' with the result that all of the enemy were either killed or taken prisoner.

"Nothwithstanding the proximity of the enemy, the posts were held until the stipulated time had elapsed, the men were then cleverly withdrawn without a casualty.

"It was imperative that the posts should be held in order to cover the approach of a large advance. The coolness, bravery, and skilful leadership displayed brought the enterprise to a successful issue.

"On the following day, this same N.C.O., seeing two enemy scouts approaching our Line, went out and waylaid them. He shot one and took the other prisoner.

"Throughout his long service with the Battalion, he proved himself a skilful, fearless leader, who had shown an excellent example to his men."

WE CARRY ON

We now set to work to strengthen our lines of defence. Dugouts were improved and we made it reasonably safe for our travelling cookers and ration limbers to draw right up as far as Battalion Headquarters.

Our patrols continued to be very active and established themselves as "masters of No-man's Land."

A lull in the fighting operations started on March 31st. We then found the Australian Fifth Division to be on our right flank, alongside the River Somme. The Fifth Division had taken over part of the line which had been held by our A Company.

HEILLY

On April 1st, we went out of the line for a little while, our relief was completed by midnight, without any interference on the part of the enemy. We bivouacked in the valley north of the village of Vaux, having the

43rd Battalion on our left flank, and the 52nd Battalion on our right, over the Somme River.

Our headquarters were at Heilly, in an old brickfield. Nearby was a tall chimney stack which was used by the enemy as a registering mark for his gunners. The brickfield in consequence became a very unhealthy spot. There was, however, a wood close handy, where a deep gravel pit existed. This place was tunnelled by us, and there our headquarters were safely established.

Our working parties never ceased operating. They were occupied in a variety of ways, among which was the building of emplacements for anti-aircraft guns.

The enemy, on April 4th advanced on the British line in the vicinity of Hamel, then held by British Regiments, which were driven out of their trenches at 11 o'clock in the morning.

Our artillery was so placed, however, that heavy enfilade fire could be poured on the advancing enemy, and great execution was done to his troops.

Our observation from the high ground enabled us to view the entire enemy operation. It was some time before we could grasp and realise the fact that British troops were actually withdrawing from before Hamel Village and Bouzancourt, immediately on our right flank. By this, the enemy was allowed to make a gain of 3000 yards, which brought him to the eastern outskirts of Villers-Bretonneux, a gain which three months later cost the Australian Forces a supreme effort in order to compel him to surrender it.

The possibility of such a withdrawal from these positions had not been overlooked by our generals. A Battalion of the 15th Australian Infantry Brigade was protecting the canal and River Somme and bridges from Bouzancourt to Corbie. A strong protective flank was thus provided for our positions north of the river.

Our A Company, which was attached to the 44th Battalion, sustained some casualties along the Somme Canal and between Sailly le Sec and Vaux.

The next day, April 5th, it rained heavily. A fierce attack was launched on the Australian Fourth Divisional troops opposite Dernancourt, where they occupied the high ground. After severe fighting, during which heavy losses were inflicted upon the enemy, he was completely repulsed.

It was well for us that he did not succeed, for had he captured those heights, the whole Third Division must have inevitably been withdrawn. Our working parties were engaged digging reserve line trenches in the vicinity of the Corbie-Bray Road, during which they were subjected to shelling by high explosive mixed with gas, due to which several casualties were sustained.

We had the satisfaction of seeing an enemy plane brought down near to our bivouac. Both pilot and observer were killed.

ACTIVITY IN THE AIR

Aerial combats now became a frequent source of excitement to us. Up to this time the enemy had adopted a sort of passive defence, but now he suddenly completely reversed his attitude. On April 6th, he made a determined effort to obtain mastery of the air. He met with very dubious success, for when he sent up several triplanes they were immediately attacked by our own planes. There was great excitement as three planes were seen to fall in flames. Two others were shot down, whilst many others were compelled to make forced landings. The losses, unfortunately, were not confined to the enemy, for a few of those disabled planes happened to belong to us.

TRENCH FEET

On April 7th, we took over from the 44th Battalion, and were supported on the left by the 43rd, whilst on our right, over the Somme River was the 49th Battalion of the Fourth Australian Division. The 44th Battalion left two platoons behind which were attached to us for the time being.

Although the weather was cold and wet, and we were without cover of any description overhead, it was really wonderful how cheerful we were under such adverse conditions.

Foot trouble, or trench feet as it was generally termed, was somewhat prevalent at this time and strict orders were issued by Divisional Headquarters to the effect that our men must have their feet rubbed and every precaution taken to prevent the spreading of the complaint. We continued to hold the line until April 13th, when we retired to the valley north of Vaux for a brief respite. During our occupancy of the line we had two trench-martars installed on our front and a new dugout was started in Shrapnel Alley for future Battalion Headquarters.

NEWS OF THE FALL OF ARMENTIERES

Whilst we were holding up the German advance in the Somme area, the enemy's anticipated attack on the Flanders Front eventuated. The lull in operations which had occurred in our region enabled him to transfer his attentions to the northern sector, where he carried out his efforts with considerable success.

Armentieres had fallen into his hands and he was rapidly advancing on Bailluel.

Our First Australian Division, which had reached the Somme only a few days earlier, was hurriedly despatched to the north again in an endeavour to stem the advance of the enemy towards the Channel Ports. Our gallant comrades carried out their mission with the utmost success, and thus again were German aspirations frustrated by Australian troops.

Nevertheless, it caused us many pangs of keen regret when we learnt of the large amount of territory the enemy had re-taken. We should not have been human had we been otherwise than enraged when we contemplated how vain had been rendered all the vast amount of energy we had expended on defences. We thought of the miles of barbed-wire entanglements we had laid; the concrete dugouts we had built, the gun positions we had erected. All these works we had performed to defend the ground desperately won at the expense of lives of some of our best friends and comrades.

COMPANY COMMANDER KILLED

Whilst out of the line a serious misfortune happened to the Battalion. The enemy, indulging in one of his regular "area shoots" was on April 16th, searching for our artillery positions in the vicinity of our Battalion. Stray shells caused us some casualties, and resulted in the death of the highly-esteemed and very capable Commander of D Company, when on his way to Battalion Headquarters.

TRENCH WARFARE AGAIN

We returned to the trenches at Sailly le Sec on April 19. Our activities now dwindled down to the old familiar "trench warfare." But living in this new system of trenches did not, however, seem so monotonous to us as did the trench life in Flanders and other places in Northern France where we had sojourned for just on eighteen months previously.

Still, back again came the same old routine of "working parties," bearing in its train the same old fatigues of carrying, wiring, digging and filling sand-bags.

SMALL RAIDING PARTIES

We now began to make the enemy very "jumpy" by employing a system of continuous raiding. His nervousness was apparent from the extravagant use he made of his Verey lights.

Our raiding parties consisted of only 1 officer and 20 other ranks. These raids were supported by an artillery barrage which commenced as an "area shoot," and subsequently developed into a light "box-barrage," which covered the particular enemy post to be raided. Under cover of the noise and confusion the small raiding party rushed the post, took prisoner all who surrendered and killed those who resisted.

FURTHER AERIAL ACTIVITY

April 21st was a day of great aerial activity, and witnessed the ending of the career and exploits of the most interpid of all the enemy's airmen, namely, Baron von Richthofen. According to the 11th Brigade records, he was brought down and killed by fire from Lewis gunners of the Fourth Australian Division.

BONNAY

Some considerable time had now elapsed since we had enjoyed the luxury of regular baths. We greatly appreciated, therefore, the novelty of going to the newly-established baths which were situated in the village of Bonnay. But no sooner had we started a revival of cleanly habits than the village became subjected to particularly heavy shelling. On April the 24th, high explosive shells mixed with gas were sent over by the enemy in such profusion and density as to force our B Eschelon, which was established at Bonnay, to hurriedly evacuate and take up a defensive position North of the River Ancre.

A rain of shells fell on the entire Battalion area. Starting at 6 a.m. the bombardment inflicted casualties upon us to the extent of 12 killed and 35 wounded. This was the prelude to an attack in force by the enemy, which, however, did not fall on our part of the line.

VILLERS-BRETONNEUX

It was Villers-Bretonneux that the enemy attacked and gained possession of. At that time it was held by a weak and exhausted British Regiment. But the Germans were not permitted to remain long in their newly-acquired domain, for at 10 o'clock that same night, the 13th and 14th Australian Brigades counter-attacked and succeeded in re-capturing all the ground which had been lost earlier in the day. When dawn broke next day, which happened to be the third anniversary of Anzac Day, it found Australian troops in full possession of the town of Villers-Bretonneux.

But the enemy did not abandon all hope of re-taking this important strategical position, until he had made repeated costly but unsuccessful attempts. In spite of all his many efforts, Villers-Bretonneux remainded in our hands until the termination of the War.

Hence onwards, until the end of April we experienced a somewhat quiet time, that is, quiet to what we were used to.

We saw very few Germans, but it was quite evident they did not fail to see us, for we sustained several losses due to enemy snipers.

We went to a new sector on April 25th where we carried on extensive patrolling until relieved in that location by the 33rd Battalion, and then we marched to a bivouac, prior to going to La Houssaye for a rest. Earlier in the month our strength was 51 officers and 1008 other ranks. This was reduced at the end of the month to 49 officers and 967 other ranks.

A WELL-EARNED RESPITE

At the beginning of the month of May, it was decided that all units of the Third Division should be withdrawn for a brief rest. Ever since the momentous rush down to the Somme from Northern France, which started on March 22nd, our Battalion had been continuously employed.

Accordingly, at dusk on May 1st, we moved out en route for La Houssaye, which village was reached at midnight, when we billeted and partook of a most appreciated meal.

The route traversed was an emergency track over the River Ancre, East of Bonnay.

We spent several days in La Houssaye during which a good deal of attention was given to further training, for whilst in the line for any length of time, ordinary routine was relaxed, and this rendered it necessary for us to get into training again at the earliest possible moment.

Our Heads saw to it that this matter was seldom, or rather never, overlooked.

The weather was excellent and we were in the best of spirits. Although some considerable time had elapsed since we had openly paid attention to our religious duties, most of us had in privacy given much time and thought in this direction. Sunday, May 5th, gave us the opportunity of attending a church parade, which was availed of by practically every man.

But we had no sooner got used to La Houssaye and began to like the place than we were ordered to prepare to move off. Accordingly we left La Houssaye behind on May 9th, at 11 in the morning. Querrieu was our destination. We halted on the way there at a place called Pont Noyelles.

We took over billets from the 25th Australian Battalion at 7 p.m., and for a few days spent our time as pleasantly as conditions would allow. We indulged in the usual training and had many sports gatherings, when various competitions and races excited considerable interest.

BOIS L'ABBE (ABBEY WOOD)
VILLERS-BRETONNEUX

We were inspected on May 17th by the Commander-in-Chief of the British Forces, General Sir Douglas Haig, who expressed himself favourably impressed by the men of the 11th Brigade.

The following day we were on the move again and established ourselves in the La Houssaye switch line. Here we remained until the 20th of May, when we received orders to march to the now famous town of

Villers-Bretonneux. We left at 1.30 p.m., travelling through Daours and eventually relieved the 15th Battalion in reserve lines at 10 p.m. Our headquarters were established at La Motte-Brebiere. We were employed in improving the defences of the support and communicating trenches.

On May 23rd, our front line was advanced by digging a succession of posts. Our A Company relieved a company of the Pioneer Battalion in the town defences of Villers-Bretonneux and, for the time being, came under the command of the O.C. 44th Battalion.

SERIOUS GAS ATTACKS

The next day, May 24th, a heavy artillery duel was heard coming from the direction of Albert. The following day we were subjected to the severest and most serious gas attack in our experience.

It started at 5.30 p.m., when the enemy shelled our positions with mustard gas. For fully half an hour he poured it in. A few hours later, at 8.30, the gas bombardment recommenced and lasted for three hours. A heavy concentration of gas pervaded the atmosphere, which caused the wearing of gas-masks to be imperative and continuous. Whilst these gas-shells were coming over to us in such profusion, a very considerable number of high explosive shells were directed by the enemy on to the roads, rendering the movement of all transport a most hazardous undertaking. This naturally caused much delay in the bringing up of rations to the companies in the line. They were eventually delivered at mid-night.

Our C Company was in the defences of Villers-Bretonneux, whilst the remaining companies were employed as working parties. Next day the gas bombardment was renewed and lasted for at least three hours. For over eight hours we had worn our gas-masks, consequently it was impossible for us to get any sleep. In spite of being thus harassed we had only seven casualties, but it was when we got to our shelters that the effect of the gas became apparent.

As the day wore on, the heat of the sun drew out the fumes that had accumulated among the trees in the wood. A choppy wind then sprang up which drove clouds of gas constantly towards the sleeping men, who on awak-

AFTER A GAS ATTACK (VILLERS-BRETONNEUX, MAY, 1918)
On this occasion two Companies were rendered Casualties.

ening, found their eyes very badly affected. As time passed the ill-effects increased. Another cause of the casualties was that uniforms had become absolutely saturated with the gas which permeated the atmosphere. During the night, whilst they slept, the men inhaled fumes from their impregnated clothing. Even the doctor's orderly, who had been nowhere near the scene of the gassing, became a casualty, having inhaled a quantity of gas by merely bending over and attending to the men who were being evacuated. At the end of the day, every officer and man of A and B Companies, bivouacked in the Valley, had to be evacuated.

On May 27th, our numbers were so depleted, that it was necessary to form a composite company.

We relieved the 44th Battalion in the line, D Company took over with C Company and the "Composite" Company in supports, and on May 28th, we were in the line astride Villers-Bretonneux.

There was not a great deal of shelling in the forward areas, though our Headquarters were subjected to a heavy "Straafe" during the evening.

FRENCH ZOUAVES

Up to this time we had not met any French soldiers, with the exception of those we became acquainted with when "On Leave," or in the estaminets. In the sector we now occupied, we came across many of them. They were called Zouaves. They came around to exchange greetings with us, but as they could not talk our language and, in spite of the months we had been in France, our knowledge of French was still limited to a jargon known as "Digger French," it was not possible to hold lengthy conversations. Yet withal, a mutual understanding and appreciation was established in semi-silence between these French troops and ourselves, far more eloquent than words could have achieved.

IN THE QUARRY

Our location on May 29th, was known as "The Quarry," and whilst here two German soldiers walked into our lines, having lost their bearings. We naturally made them prisoners to which they appeared to have not the slightest objection.

We made improvements in our outpost lines by connecting the posts and placing fire-bays therein.

During the last two days of the month of May, Villers-Bretonneux was subjected to severe shelling, demolishing many of the buildings which had thus far escaped serious injury. The enemy artillery received all they were looking for in the way of "reciprocity" at the hands of our Australian gunners.

MAJOR GENERAL GELLIBRAND TAKES COMMAND OF THE THIRD DIVISION

On May 30th, General Monash, who up to this time was in command of the Third Australian Division, assumed command of the newly-formed Australian Army Corps, thence onward the Third Division became under the command of Major-General Gellibrand.

In his farewell order to the Third Division General Monash states:—

> "I find it impossible to give adequate expression to my feelings of gratitude towards all ranks for the splendid and loyal support which you have at all times accorded me . . . .
>
> "It is my earnest hope, and also my sincere conviction, that the fine spirit and the high efficiency will be maintained under the leadership of my successor, Brigadier-General Gellibrand, and if the men of the Division feel, as I trust they do, an obligation to perpetuate for my sake, the traditions built up by them, they can do so in no better way than by rendering to him a service as thorough and a support as loyal as I have been privileged to enjoy at their hands.
>
> "In formally wishing the Division Good-bye and Good Luck, I wish simply, but none the less sincerely, to thank you one and all for all you have done."

JUNE 1918

The month of June was somewhat of a contrast to those months which had preceded it. Had we but known, we might have regarded the period as "the calm which presages a storm." The weather throughout was remarkably good.

During the first four days we were engaged in front

of Villers-Bretonneux. Our A Company was now a Composite Company. The 49th Battalion had a company supporting us on the right and another company in charge of the defences of the town. This arrangement was rendered necessary on account of the serious number of casualties which were inflicted upon us by gas on May 26th.

On the second day of the month the enemy gave us another taste of gas. This time it was phosgene that he put over. No less than two thousand rounds of this gas fell in the area occupied by us. It was remarkable that no casualties eventuated therefrom.

WE ARE VISITED BY THE PRIME MINISTERS OF FRANCE AND AUSTRALIA.

We this day received a visit from Monsieur Clemenceau, the Prime Minister of France, who accompanied our own Prime Minister of Australia the Right Honourable William Morris Hughes, familiarly known to the troops as Billy Hughes, who subsequently addressed us and complimented us upon our fine work and morale, making generous promises of rest and comforts that were to come our way.

Just before midnight of June 4th, we were relieved and whilst the operation was in progress our approaches to and from the line were severely straafed. Eventually we arrived at our new location, which was a railway cutting known as "Number 28," and here our Battalion became part of a reserve brigade. We enjoyed the luxury of frequent bathing in the River Somme, but training and the everlasting "fatigues" and working-parties continued unabated. We remained in this locality until the twenty-third day of the month when we relieved the 40th Battalion in Abbey Wood, our Headquarters being at what was called "The White Chateau."

After a lapse of a few days we were in turn relieved on the 27th, on which day our Battalion Commander, who had been acting Brigadier-General, returned to the Battalion.

We marched to the Reserve Brigade Area at Blangy Tronville, prior to setting out for Allonville Wood on the following day. Owing to the frequency of bombing attacks, at Allonville, it was found necessary to sink all bivouacs at least two feet below the surface to afford shelter from the fragments of metal.

THE TANKS AND THE YANKS

The two final days of the month brought us face to face with two factors in the War with which we had hitherto little or no experience. These were The Tanks and The Yanks.

To the Tanks we were introduced on June 29th. In the quiet little village of Vaux, situated in a pleasant valley, north-west of Amiens, the tanks were made to go through their performances. They demonstrated to us what might be expected of them. As we got better acquainted with these monsters, so our confidence in them increased. We gradually grew more familiar with the habits of these strange, uncanny huge masses of machanism and placed reliance on their support.

As for the Yanks, our first glimpse of the American Army came along with the last day of the month. A few platoons of Yanks reported to us for experience to enable them to take part in the next stunt. They exhibited great keenness and were appreciative listeners. The strength of the Battalion had by this time dwindled down to 33 officers and 669 other ranks.

PREPARATIONS FOR THE BATTLE OF HAMEL

When July dawned it found the 42nd Battalion busily engaged organising and preparing for the stunt which we instinctively knew would be carried out very shortly. Our new friends, the Yanks, had been taken over in lorries to Vaux-sur Somme, in order to let them get acquainted with the tanks.

On July 2nd, we abandoned our "homes" in the rest area at Allonville, and marched via Querrieu and Pont Noyelles to Bussey le Daours where we had a hot meal. After a couple of hours rest we continued the journey to the line, marching through Daours and then alongside the Somme until the village of Hamlet was reached. Here we were met by guides who directed us into the Hamel sector.

Our occupation was completed by midnight. Battalion Headquarters were established in Shrapnel Gully in conjunction with the 46th Battalion. Next day, the 3rd of

July, we were resting in the trenches. Hot meals were supplied to us, but on account of the forthcoming operation, which was to be sprung as a complete surprise upon the enemy, movement of every description had to be reduced to a minimum.

AMERICAN TROOPS WITHDRAWN

It was the general belief, that as a compliment to our American Allies, the day chosen for the assault would probably be July 4th, American Independence Day. This surmise turned out to be correct. It was, therefore, a sore disappointment to us when we learnt that three out of the five companies of U.S.A. troops, which had been attached to our 11th Brigade, would not take part. But we could not blame the men who comprised those companies for they were, if possible, even more disappointed than we, for this was to have been their first real battle, but orders had to be obeyed.

This alteration of plans necessitated more than a considerable amount of re-adjustment of troops. Here at the eleventh hour, the attacking force had to be re-organised at practically a moment's notice. The withdrawal of these 750 men left the Brigade with only 2,200 men instead of just on 3000 as had been expected.

Only four platoons of Americans took part with our Battalion in the Hamel stunt. A composite company had to be made up hastily from our C Eschelon in order to replace the American troops which had been withdrawn. The front allotted to the 42nd Battalion was from the south bank of the Somme to the road north of Hamel.

THE BATTLE OF HAMEL

The whole offensive was under the charge of General McLagan of the 4th Division. One brigade each from the 2nd, 3rd, and 4th Divisions took part. The 11th Brigade was chosen from the 3rd Division.

As soon as darkness permitted the assembly, tapes were laid down by our scout officer, and at 2 a.m. the entire Battalion was on the line without the slightest hitch. Preparations were all complete, and the remaining time, up to zero hour was reasonably quiet, excepting that at eight minutes prior to zero hour, our artillery put up a tremendously heavy harassing fire upon all the enemy positions.

This was all part of a plan. For several nights past, our artillery had been sending over a regular and organised "shoot" which must have created in the mind of the enemy that it was just one of our bad habits. On this occasion, however, the roar of our guns was utilised as a means of drowning the noise of the tanks as they took up their positions.

Waiting in No-man's Land on assembly lines was always a time of tension. Our men well knew the danger and seriousness of the work to be carried out, and that upon their silence depended the success of the enterprise. Cigarettes were rolled, during these anxious moments, and immediately the order to advance was given, matches were struck, cigarettes puffed, as the troops went forward courageously and unperturbed.

On July 4th, at 3.10 a.m. our offensive opened with a mighty artillery barrage, which fell in No-man's Land, 400 yards east of our front line. The whole atmosphere seemed almost alight with gun flashes. Immediately the artillery started the harassing fire, the tanks began to move forward from their assembly point and continued the movement whilst the guns were roaring, so that by zero time they were well forward. In all thirty-five tanks were employed; thirty-three fighters and two supply tanks.

The barrage crept up in lifts up to 600 yards beyond the objective, where it remainded for one hour.

No sooner had the barrage lifted than we all went forward with confidence as though going on a route march, and this greatly amused our companions from America. By the time we had made our first halt, the tanks were well up with us. They then went forward in advance, attacking machine-gun positions and other strong points.

Whilst this was transpiring, an enemy tank appeared upon the scene. It made for one of our tanks which had been partially disabled. When quite close, the enemy tank brought its gun into action, and missed. Our tank turned in time to avoid trouble, just as another of our tanks came to its rescue, bumping the Hun tank severely and setting it on fire. The Hun tank, much discomforted, made a bolt for it and scooted hurriedly to the rear of Accroche Wood, where it was last seen in a badly burnt condition.

The work of our tanks was astonishing. No obstacle could impede their progress. It was soon discovered that it was possible for infantry commanders to "speak" to the tanks, and direct their movements towards strong points which were holding up the infantry. Their antics were most amusing, especially so the spectacle of one of them rounding up parties of the enemy who had been sheltering in shell-holes, and then sending them back as prisoners.

During our advance, several enemy machine-guns caused trouble. In one instance, three members of one of our Lewis-gun crews were knocked out. One of the crew who was uninjured, out-flanked the German machine-gun, and by the aid of Mills bombs and his bayonet, succeeded in getting the entire enemy machine-gun crew.

In another instance, a party went to attack a heavy machine-gun which was causing us much trouble. Just as the job was about completed, the officer in charge of the party was killed, when a private carried on in spite of a severe leg wound. This private rushed the machine-gun, his strength was almost spent, but it lasted sufficiently long to enable him to bayonet the enemy gunner. He then fell unconscious without being able to extract the bayonet.

The Americans worked well and gave excellent service. Their admiration for the Australian soldier was unbounded. We, on our part, equally reciprocated those sentiments.

Our companies subsequently established themselves in what had so recently been the Headquarters of the enemy. Set out in them, we found numerous documents and maps. There was also an abundance of food which had evidently been only recently delivered.

The enemy was apparently paralysed by the suddenness of our assault, for little trouble was experienced from his field artillery which must have been hastily withdrawn.

Neither, during the day, did he make any serious attempts to retaliate by way of counter-attacks. Our patrols, on the contrary, were very active and searched every locality likely to afford cover. They "mopped-up" as they went. The number of prisoners they sent back was evidence of the completeness with which the job was executed.

At dusk, however, the 11th Brigade had to withstand a very determined counter-attack. The enemy made a strenuous effort to regain the lost territory, but he was driven off with heavy loss. The remainder of the night passed quietly, except upon the adjoining Battalion front, where a "strong point" which had not been mopped-up caused a lot of trouble. Eventually this was dealt with most effectively.

July 5th found the enemy feeling his way back again, and our front line was subjected to heavy "straafing" at intervals.

Our total casualties in this operation were: Two officers and one other ranks killed; forty-eight other ranks wounded. The American losses were: Two officers and three other ranks wounded.

At midnight, July 5th, we were relieved and moved to La Neuville. Here we bivouacked and had breakfast preparatory to marching to Daours, where we were met by omnibuses which conveyed us to Allonville, which was reached by 1 o'clock p.m. on July 6th. The Battalion had been away exactly four days. The band played us in.

News of the good work we had accomplished had long since been passed back and much appreciation and many congratulations were expressed by members of neighbouring units who had assembled to greet us.

WE PART WITH THE AMERICANS

When our bivouac area was reached, the Americans, with much demur, realised that their association with us must now end. Many a short-lived friendship was thus severed but never entirely forgotten.

The Americans expressed a one and only wish, namely, "that they might be allowed always to remain with the Australians." The men of the platoon of Americans which had been withdrawn at the last moment, were filled with lamentations and made no secret of their disappointment. It might be mentioned that several of them tried various ruses which they thought would enable them to enter the stunt. It is known that in at least two instances, American privates borrowed Australian uniforms and as camouflaged Diggers realised their ambitions. These troops belonged to the 131st American Battalion.

EULOGIES AND MESSAGES OF CONGRATULATION

On the completion of the operation eulogistic expressions were duly received from Brigade, Divisional and Army Commanders, as well as from General Headquarters. Praiseworthy and congratulatory messages were forwarded by the Prime Minister of Great Britain, the Prime Minister of Australia, who was then in London, and a day later, from our own people in Australia through the Governor-General.

As to the gains due to this operation, the final calculations were as follows:—

1500 prisoners, including 60 officers.
150 machine-guns.
73 Minenwerfer guns, light and heavy.
2000 rifles.
100 scout pistols.

A wireless set and a considerable amount of equipment, tools and material.

THE WORK OF THE AIR FORCE

Any account of the Battle of Hamel would be incomplete without reference to the work of the Air Force, which throughout maintained supremacy of the air. For the first time in warfare, ammunition in boxes was delivered to the gunners in the forward area by aeroplanes, and food supplies were dropped by the same means.

EXCELLENT WORK BY ALL SERVICES

Medical and signal services were both of them excellently maintained. They stood up to the strain of continuous calls, in fact, there was not one branch, arm or detail, that did not carry out all the duties assigned with a precision bordering upon perfection.

A BRIEF RESPITE AT ALLONVILLE

July 6th, found us indulging in sports in the Woods of Allonville. Of course, the usual training was not forgotten, and though we should have preferred to spend a much longer time in those peaceful and picturesque surroundings, after a week's residence, we were called upon to get on the move again.

Allonville presented itself to us as a typical French estate. There was a particularly fine chateau nestling among the trees which we were given to understand was the country residence of the Hennessy's of Three Star Brandy fame.

Our transfer took us to the Hamel sector. Here on July 17th, during the early hours of the morning, the enemy peppered us with mustard gas. Although he gave us a very generous issue, effective treatment prevented casualties, whilst a fall of rain fortunately cleared the atmosphere very considerably.

We remained in this sector until August 4th, when we proceeded to Corbie. Here we were shown a complete replica of the ground over which our next stunt was to be performed. The exact date was kept a profound secret from us. It was, however, quite evident that the time for the "hop-over" was not far distant. Comprehensive re-fitting and re-equipment were sufficient indications. Our "rest" was now over. The 42nd Battalion was once again ready and alert, straining like a greyhound on the leash.

At length, on August 8th, the curtain went up upon the first scene of what transpired to be "the Last Act" of the Great War.

Enterprise

The Great Push, August the Eighth—The Daylight Stunt
—Happy Valley—Mont St. Quentin—Tincourt

The Great Push, August the Eighth.

Termed by the enemy, "Germany's Black Day," the Eighth of August stands out in bold relief as the brightest in the Australian annals of the War.

It was at 3.30 (one hour before zero) that we assembled on our "jumping-off tape." We were all fresh and fit. The movement was carried out without the slightest hitch or hesitation.

With the arrival of zero hour (4.20 a.m.) our artillery opened out with a deafening crash, to which the enemy artillery lost no time in responding.

We infantry started forward immediately, accompanied by the huge prodigies of mechanism called tanks, with which we now considered ourselves on terms of familiarity. Here we were together; those immense ungainly, uncanny monsters and ourselves, moving forward in unison through the early morning gloom, a gloom that was intensified by a dense heavy fog. This fog rendered observation almost impossible, and caused much difficulty in maintaining direction and keeping touch. But at the same time it had its advantages. It prevented the enemy from observing our movements.

The attack of our Battalion, which was Left Flank Battalion of the Australian Corps, was directed along the south bank of the River Somme, on a frontage of 750 yards. The 44th Battalion was on our South Flank, whilst the 41st Battalion was in support and the 43rd Battalion in reserve.

When the 42nd and 44th Battalions had reached a position 400 yards east of the Gailly-Warfusse Road, the 41st Battalion leap-frogged through the 44th Battalion and joined us in the advance.

We advanced to Cerisy-Gailly, where a bridge crossed

the Somme and enabled us to link up with troops on North Bank, in fact, one company from the 9th Brigade was allotted to the 42nd Battalion, to advance on the North Bank of the Somme and so make contact with us at Cerisy-Gailly.

At Warfusse-Gailly, which was a small town where temporary buildings had been erected by the Germans, we found and captured a casualty clearing station or hospital.

The attack was pressed home according to plan. The enemy surrendered to us in large numbers and our first objective was reached by 7.30 a.m., and then the work of consolidation began.

Battalion Headquarters were established at Warfusse-Gailly at 8.30 a.m. The Battalion cookers were brought to this point and a hot breakfast was served to the men in the front line before 9 o'clock. This was considered a remarkable achievement, as never before had the cookers been so close to the front line in an attack.

So successful was our "breaking through" of the enemy's defences that the plan for the Fourth Division to leap-frog through our lines was carried out without a hitch. It was a magnificent sight to watch the troops, followed by artillery, travel over the ground we had just recently captured, and as we relaxed a little to get some of our breath back, we witnessed the advance and continuance of the general offensive.

A British Brigade on our Left Flank met with only partial success. This rendered our Left Flank exposed to enemy enfilade fire, which caused us many casualties.

But we had a great day. We took three hundred prisoners, captured three '77 guns, 25 machine-guns, 7 trench-mortars, and a large quantity of ammunition and stores, all at a cost of but few casualties. Our Battalion Headquarters were established in a locality which only a matter of seven hours previous had been well behind the enemy's front line.

The following day we rested in the position we then occupied, and on August 10th were ordered to take over from the 14th Battalion at Morcourt. The disposition of the 11th Brigade was as follows:—

The 41st Battalion on the right, 43rd on the left, with the 42nd in support and the 44th in reserve. The

PREPARING SOUVENIRED POULTRY FOR THE "BABBLING BROOKS."

11th Machine-gun Company with its sixteen guns along with the 11th Trench-Mortars, assisted each of the Battalions. We were now in the vicinity of Proyart.

It had been decided that the 10th Brigade would advance our line, but a flight of enemy bombing planes threw the 10th Brigade into confusion and its Commander was killed. This caused the 9th and 11th Brigades to be sent up in order to reinforce. During the following day all three brigades completed the operation by possessing themselves of the villages of Morcourt and Proyart, and the woods adjoining the River Somme.

During August 11th, arrangements were made for the 41st Battalion to attack and capture portion of the Amiens line, south of the Somme, which at that time was not held by us. The attack went well, but enemy machine-guns remained active throughout. After a hard fight the whole line was captured. As the 41st Battalion moved to the attack, the 42nd advanced and took over the southern portion of the Brigade front, which that night was extended southwards. The 42nd was on the right, the 41st on the left, the 44th right support, and the 43rd left support.

THE DAYLIGHT STUNT

The twelfth of August was the day on which we performed what has ever since been referred to as "The Daylight Stunt."

Commencing with daylight, the area was mopped up by 7.0 a.m. The 10th Brigade reported their patrols were east of Proyart. The 42nd and 43rd Battalions were ordered to establish themselves in assigned positions. The 42nd immediately sent out patrols and became engaged with the enemy, who was strongly holding St. Germains Wood. By a flanking movement, we captured that Wood along with something like sixty prisoners. For this attack we had no assistance from the artillery.

The general advance continued, but on account of the strong position encountered, our progress was slow, and this retardment was accentuated by the misunderstanding of a verbal message, whereby the operation of troops which should have supported us on the left, did not materialise until a later time than had been planned, and this, for a while, rendered our left flank exposed.

Throughout all this fighting, enemy artillery fired heavily upon our newly acquired territory, mixing gas along with high explosive shells.

During the operation we were assisted by three platoons of the 44th Battalion which acted as carrying parties in the afternoon. Prisoners were brought in to the number of one hundred and ten. To have attacked such a position in broad daylight was to demand a very high standard of leadership as well as courage and efficiency on the part of all ranks.

Our men responded to the demands made upon them in every way, and the day's exploit resulted in a success, and this success was attributed to the irresistible dash and spirit of all concerned.

But at the same time, it has to be confessed, we suffered many casualties, quite fifty per cent. of which were caused by enemy artillery fire, indicating that although the enemy had been allowed only extremely limited time in which to organise his artillery, our attack in broad daylight, without the aid of artillery, proved a costly undertaking.

Many of the enemy were seen in Long and Lug Woods, which gave the impression that he intended to counter-attack. In expectation of such a move, both our heavy and field artilleries were directed upon his concentration of troops, and this evidently prevented the development of any proposed counter-attack.

At mid-night we handed over to the Sherwood Foresters, and moved back to our old positions around Cerisy-Gailly. The following few days were utilised in re-fitting and training. In this region, in such proximity to the River Somme, advantage was taken of every opportunity that afforded the luxury of a bathe and a swim.

It was on the 19th of the month that we moved across the Somme in order to execute some mopping-up work in an area that badly needed such attention.

A few days later we were at Reveille Farm, where Dame Nature staged a magnificent turn for us. Here we witnessed a most wonderful display of moonlight which turned the nocturnal hours into perfect daylight. But any flights into the realms of fancy which we might have been tempted to indulge in, were instantly dispelled when at 4.45 a.m. our barrage opened, bringing our minds back with a jerk to grim reality.

Three-quarters of an hour later we were moving forward again and advanced through our battery positions where the noise of the guns almost deafened us. The din from the massed artillery exceeded the limits of even the most powerful imagination.

As our companies arrived they took up positions in shell-holes recently vacated by the 33rd Battalion. Our Headquarters were established in tunnels, which only a short time prior had been occupied by the enemy.

The weather changed next day. It was intensely hot, and to add to our discomfort, the enemy drenched the wood we occupied, called Bois de Tailles, with phosgene and sneezing gas, with which were mixed quantities of high explosive shells.

Owing to troops on the left having retired from their objectives, our Battalion was immediately disposed for the north flank protection of the 11th Brigade. The objectives on the left were eventually regained on August 24th, on which day the village of Bray was taken by the 10th Brigade.

HAPPY VALLEY

Our advance still continued over the country which so recently had been in the enemy's hands. The locality over which our operations now spread is usually referred to as Happy Valley.

The nights of bright moonlight continued, and the weather remained warm, often unbearably hot, whilst at all times we were subjected to heavy shell fire, causing us to seek shelter and protection in shell-holes, wherein during daylight, we sometimes remained for long periods. When darkness fell, we dug in and consolidated our positions.

We were still closely following up the retreating enemy, who on August 26th, was observed vacating in disorder his position in Vaux Wood. His artillery, however was very alert, so that any undue movement on our part resulted in immediate shelling in our vicinity. But the activity of his artillery subsided considerably towards evening.

At 7 p.m. we received orders to move forward through

the 44th Battalion and take up a position in advance. These orders were subsequently altered, our C Company being used as reserve to the 41st Battalion, which made the advance, the other three companies were held in reserve. The Battalion was acting under command of the 44th Battalion during most of this operation.

PRAISE FOR THE COOKS

A word of praise might here be recorded for the work of the "Babbling Brooks" the term by which the cooks were always known throughout the Australian Army, for the manner in which they attended to the requirements of their comrades in the front line. Two hot meals were taken forward daily during this stunt, by mess-orderlies who cheerfully carried out their duties.

MONT ST. QUENTIN STUNT

Our Brigade was relieved by the 9th Brigade, and on August 28th, we rested. Our equipment and organisation were checked and this naturally meant that some fresh activity was about to be launched. The expected order for a forward movement arrived soon after 9 a.m. on August 29th, then off we marched once more to trail the Hun. A few hours later we were occupying the Maricourt-Suzanne Valley, and for the time being, came under the command of the 9th Brigade. The reason for this was that the 35th Battalion (9th Brigade) had sustained so many casualties that it had to be placed in reserve at Fargny Mill.

The 9th Brigade's line extended as far as Curlu, which at that time was the name for just a heap of brick-dust, though it was formerly a very flourishing village.

We were now entering that area which had been devastated by the enemy during the years of the earlier Somme battles. On August 30th, we took up a position in Hindley Wood, previously occupied by the 33rd Battalion. Here we remained until the early hours of the morning of the 31st, when at 3 a.m. our B Company moved up behind the 33rd Battalion, which had met with stubborn resistance on the part of the enemy.

So determined was the stand he made, that it was necessary for the Commanding Officer of the 33rd Battalion to call upon his reserve company (which was B company of the 42nd) in order to gain his objective. Desperate hand to hand fighting took place in the maze of trenches with which the locality abounded.

Ample testimony of the fierce resistance put up by the enemy on this occasion was to be gained by the sight of the large numbers of dead Prussian Guards of the picked regiment called "The Kaiserin Augusta Grenadier Guards," whose bodies lay where they fell at their posts, due to the effects of our bombing and Lewis-gun and rifle fire. These Prussian Guards were fresh troops which had been hastily despatched to this front in an endeavour to stem the tide of success that was carrying us on to victory.

Our B Company went in with a strength of 63 all ranks, and at 3 p.m. it had a total of merely forty men.

Three enemy planes dropped forty or more bombs in the vicinity of our bivouac, but beyond causing us to extinguish all lights and making us feel a bit breezy, no damage was sustained.

The operations which took place on the first day of September are generally referred to as "The Mont St. Quentin Stunt."

Late on the night of August 31st, a conference of Commanding Officers was held at the Headquarters of the 11th Brigade, which were situated in dugouts quite recently occupied by German troops. These along with a splendid engineering dump and general supplies of materials and artillery ammunition of all calibres, had fallen into our hands.

When the relief of the 9th Brigade was carried out, our B Company which had been in action with the 33rd Battalion was instructed by patrols to report back to Battalion Headquarters and rejoin the Battalion, which had now again become under command of our own, the 11th Brigade. This arrangement enabled B Company to get a good hot meal before the barrage opened.

The 42nd advanced to some sunken roads, with C Company on the north, D Company south, and A Company in support.

Our bombardment started at 5.30 a.m. The attacking waves got off splendidly. The enemy had already received a terrible mauling at the hands of our B Company and the 33rd Battalion, and our intense barrage added to his discomfiture.

On catching sight of the 42nd men advancing, his demoralisation seemed to become complete. When we arrived, the enemy's troops were ready to give themselves up. With the exception of some few isolated instances, the surrenders were made hastily and with scarcely any attempt at defence. Prisoners totalling 300 were sent back from the 42nd and 41st positions one hour after the attack was launched. They were in appearance some of the finest types of German troops we had yet encountered.

Our artillery barrage died down in order to allow us to exploit our gain to the fullest extent, but when the guns ceased to fire it seemed that the morale of the enemy's troops stiffened as he managed to get a little of his breath back again. But we did not allow him much time for respiration or recuperation. It was not long before our Lewis gunners and riflemen played havoc with the hastily retiring enemy troops. We also utilised many of the captured German machine-guns, which we reversed and made them to fire upon their former owners.

INSTANCES OF ENEMY HEROISM AND ADAPTABILITY

It must not be thought for one moment that all the German troops were panic-stricken. There were, indeed, many instances of extreme bravery and devotion to duty on the part of sections of the enemy, some of which are worthy of being recorded, such, for instance, of two batteries of '77's, which gamely pulled out and retired, miraculously escaping the showers of bullets that followed them, and of two other gun-teams, equally brave but not so fortunate. No sooner were the latter observed galloping off, than they were dealt with by Lewis gunners of our right platoon and of the left platoon 41st Battalion, so that neither guns, horses nor drivers got any further.

At dusk, our relief by the 12th Somerset Regiment was commenced, and completed by 1.30 a.m.

When our companies returned to Battalion Headquarters, they were met by the cooks, along with their travelling cookers, and we were provided with a big substantial meal.

We bivouacked that night in dugouts in a valley,

which in spite of its proximity to the scene of carnage, looked very beautiful under the crystal clear starlight. The air, too, was decidedly crisp and chilly, being in marked contrast to the continuous hot, balmy weather we had recently experienced.

MEDICAL OFFICER, ORDERLIES, STRETCHER-BEARERS

During the day's operations the doctor and his orderlies were, as usual, unceasing in their labours.

Our medical officer, Doctor, M.O., or Quack, whatever one liked to designate him, along with a detachment of orderlies was supplied by the 11th Field Ambulance, so that a doctor and his staff was with the Battalion at all times whether in or out of the line. The general practice was for the Battalion stretcher-bearers to bring in the wounded on stretchers, excepting in the cases of those who were termed "walking wounded." All cases were dealt with at the "Forward Dressing Station," or "First Aid Post," and given immediate attention. They were then sent on by ambulance to the nearest Casualty Clearing Station from which the worst cases were sent to the base hospitals, by Red Cross Train, and sometimes to England. In the last instance, the wound which caused evacuation to England, was termed "A Blighty," which was our nickname for England.

As for the attention given to our wounded prisoners, this was without exception equal to that given to our own men, for once a wounded man was taken prisoner, he immediately became an object for compassion, and there were few 42nd Battalion men who did not, under such conditions, share their cigarettes and rations with those who were their recent enemies.

ASSISTANCE FROM PRISONERS

The prisoners, too, deserve to be given credit for humanitarian work, for although forcibly enrolled, they carried out their duties as stretcher-bearers with willingness and alacrity.

The Aid Post, on this day, was established in a dugout situated a fair distance back, but the inconvenience of a long carry was overcome by making use of very big German ex-Guardsmen, who carried out the duties of stretcher-bearers under the surveillance of one of our own.

The new hands worked admirably, were quite docile and gave the impression that they liked their job. And so, by this means, our wounded, and the enemy's too, were speedily evacuated from the front line.

The Battalion marched off at 9 o'clock on the morning of September 2nd, and advanced due west from Clery, along the road to Curlu, on the outskirts of which we bivouacked.

The price we paid for the Mont St. Quentin Stunt was: Killed, 4 officers and 13 other ranks. Wounded: 2 officers and 48 other ranks, and two others missing.

Our gains comprised: 160 prisoners, 36 machine-guns, 3 howitzers, and ten .5 centimetre guns.

WE KEEP THE ENEMY ON THE RUN

After such strenuous times as we had experienced, it was only to be expected that we should have been utterly exhausted, and that is exactly the state we were in when the sun rose on September 4th. If there be any truth in the old saying, "There is no rest for the wicked," then the 42nd Battalion must have been a particularly bad lot, for at 11 o'clock that night instructions were received that we must prepare to move off at an hour's notice. The reason of this was that "the uninvited German visitors to France" had been observed packing up their luggage, evidently with the intention of making a hurried departure, and to the 42nd had fallen the duty of seeing those "unwelcome guests" well and securely "off the premises," and to make things so generally unpleasant for them as to give them no inducement whatsoever to alter their minds.

Accordingly, on September 5th we received orders to move to a position east of Mont St. Quentin. The route we took was along the Clery-sur-Somme Road, thence along the Mont St. Quentin Road.

THE TINCOURT STUNT

We had attached to us on this occasion, the Third Divisional Pioneer Battalion, which was allotted positions with us in the assembly line. Owing to the heat of the day and the dusty roads which were crowded with all kinds of military traffic, we found the approach march a particularly trying one. Our companies were all in position by 6 p.m. when we were given a hot meal.

Zero hour was midnight, and at 4 a.m. on September 6th all companies reported having reached their objectives, and were in touch with each other. On the right, however, our B Company and D Company of the Pioneers had met with strong resistance at Cartigny. Artillery fire was at length effective in dislodging the enemy.

On the left our D Company was unable to get in touch with the 231st Brigade, and was compelled to establish a defensive flank. It was an extremely difficult matter to keep touch on account of the intense darkness, but at no time was it lost between our companies. Use was made of patrols of the Australian Light Horse which was valuable as a protective measure.

Our advance continued with unabated energy, although at times strenuous and stubborn resistance was encountered.

Enemy artillery of all calibres was active. His machine-gun positions were numerous, and it took some hard fighting to dislodge them. On the right flank, our men on reaching the crest of the ridge, were subjected to some heavy fire from a whiz-bang battery on the opposite slope. Our artillery got on to these guns and dispersed them, but we were still harassed by enemy machine-gun fire.

Our advance was temporarly held up on account of being unable to locate troops which should have been supporting us on the right flank, also by the condition of the men, who after days and days of ceaseless activity were in a state of great fatigue.

On the left, our C and D Companies had already gained Buire Wood, but owing to heavy shelling and machine-gun fire, could not carry their advance any further.

At mid-day it was decided to put down a barrage to assist the advance, and this enabled our left companies to reach their objectives by 6 o'clock p.m., but B Company and the Pioneers on the right did not carry their advance any further.

During the morning's operations troops on the left advanced under a barrage which overlapped our boundary by about 500 yards. This caused us to move over to the right, which had the effect of squeezing out one of our companies, rendering it practically a support company.

This was unfortunate as C Company had made good Buire Wood, and upon going through it again, was subjected to severe fire from artillery and machine-guns. It was a remarkable position which the Company Commanders concerned handled well.

The strong opposition encountered by our left flank companies came from the direction of Tincourt, and later, when the ground had been captured by us, an enemy strong-post was discovered there. It consisted of two machine-gun positions, and scattered around each were three to four thousand empty machine-gun cartridge cases, which gave ample evidence of the extraordinary speed with which those bullets must have been showered upon us.

In every instance when the enemy retired he relentlessly set fire to all huts and buildings. This served him a double purpose. Firstly, the destruction of property, and secondly, to provide him with a very effective smoke screen to cover his retirement.

About midnight we were relieved by the 44th Battalion on the right and the 41st Battalion on the left. We then moved to a reserve position.

At noon, on September 7th, we moved forward two miles in support of the advancing vanguard, which this evening reached Roisel and Bernes. On the following morning, at 9 a.m., after having been relieved by the 1st Australian Brigade, we moved to a place called Doingt.

DOINGT

Not one expression of regret was heard about our being relieved. And little wonder. We had been employed in an unceasing, continuous series of operations which had depleted our ranks and left those remaining in a state of utter exhaustion.

Here, at Doingt, from the 9th to the 27th September we spent the time undergoing the regular out-of-the-line training, gradually recovering some of our lost strength. On various days we showed our prowess at football and cricket, and on the 21st took part in a sports gathering at which every unit of the 11th Brigade was represented. At nights quite a diversity of entertainment was provided for our enjoyment.

ENTERTAINMENTS AT NIGHT

The Coo-ees, the Third Divisional Concert Party, turned up with full orchestra and a galaxy of talent. They gave us good shows every night. And then we had our own 11th Brigade Concert Party called "The Blue Gums," who also enlivened the time for us. We might be pardoned for being a little biassed in favour of the Brigade "Pierrots" as they were called, on account of several 42nd men being among the entertainers.

Our Battalion was by no means lacking in musical talent, for we also supplied the "Coo-ees" with some very capable artists and musicians.

But, without doubt, of most especial interest to us were the performances put over by our enemy "Fritz." Nightly we waited with awesome expectation to listen to his crooning of "The Gotha's Hum."

Scarcely a night passed without the warning signal being heard to "put out those .... lights." Thrills of pleasure, mingled with excitement, filled our souls as we watched our searchlights seeking out those birds of ill-omen, high away up in the clouds. Immediately one was located, a concentration of dazzling beams surrounded it, making it appear like a gigantic silver moth. Strings of illuminated tracer-bullets were directed towards it from innumerable Lewis and anti-aircraft guns, to say nothing of an occasional pot-shot from one of our own Battalion snipers. We sometimes had the satisfaction of seeing one brought down in flames, but those instances were not nearly so frequent as we should have liked.

They caused little harm to our camp. Peronne seemed to be their objective, still there were very few of us who could truthfully admit they never "Got the Wind Up."

Thus recuperating, like some great fighting animal, licking its wounds after a fierce encounter, the 42nd Battalion lay quietly at Doingt, regaining its strength day by day.

AFTER RELIEF.
Returning from the Line for a Rest.

Resistance

Attempts to Extinguish the 42nd Battalion

A Terrible Blow for the Forty-Second

It was decreed that a serious calamity should fall upon our Battalion. It was threatened with extinction.

Firstly, the news was heralded by "furphies" (the Digger term for rumours). These rumours gradually grew into certainties, until finally, orders were received that the 42nd Battalion was to be broken up forthwith.

Utterances of disgust and disapproval were heard on all sides, whilst consternation surged through our ranks.

We were, all of us, set and determined that no matter what the consequences might be to ourselves as individuals, the breaking up of our splendid unit would be resisted to the uttermost. To us, it was inconceivable that the military authorities could possibly imagine that we 42nd men would calmly submit to the destruction of our Battalion; a Battalion which had covered itself with glory and distinction; a Battalion which had won unstinted praise for its trustworthiness and unflinching devotion to duty; an association which had been the means of cementing bonds of brotherly love and comradeship such as had never been exceeded in the annals of time. That we should be smashed up was unthinkable. It could not be. **It must not be.**

PREPARATION FOR RESISTANCE

Secret meetings were held. King's Regulations were studied. A resolute spirit to stick together at all costs permeated the ranks of the Battalion.

Non-Commissioned officers, and others versed in military law, drew up a plan which in due course was confided to every member of the rank and file. Secret training in this direction went on for days and nights until each of us felt strong and ready to test the power of the military machine to crush us out of existence.

It was on September 20th that the anticipated blow fell. Instructions were received that the 42nd Battalion of the 11th Infantry Brigade of the A.I.F. be disbanded and its members transferred as reinforcements to the other three Battalions of the Brigade.

September 21st was the date of the momentous parade when our Commanding Officer, who was in charge of the parade, addressed us. He expressed the utmost regret at having to carry out the decision of the High Command, and asked us to realise that the position had been created by the demands of urgent necessity.

The following commands were given and unhesitatingly obeyed: "Attention. Slope Arms. Form Fours. Right."

Upon the order to "March" being given, none but officers moved. The men stood firm as a rock.

The parade was dismissed. Routine training under N.C.O.'s was continued during the next few days. Every order issued was strictly obeyed and carried out with alacrity.

The second effort to break up the Battalion occurred on September 25th. When we paraded on this occasion it was noticed that two officers of the 41st Battalion along with the band of that unit were in attendance, evidently to escort us.

Our Commanding Officer again addressed us and exhorted us to obey orders, and to understand that it was lack of reinforcements that had rendered the breaking up of the 42nd Battalion inevitable.

Every order he gave us was promptly obeyed until we were commanded to "March." Again officers responded but not one of the rank and file made the slightest attempt to move. The officers of the 41st Battalion, along with their band, then returned to their quarters.

The following day the 42nd Battalion was reorganised. Instead of its original establishment of four companies of four platoons of sixty men, the companies were reconstructed by having only three platoons each, and the platoons consisted of only twenty-one men. We were then equipped and made ready to fight again as

"The Forty-second Battalion," in the forthcoming battle, when it was intended to take and hold the supposedly impregnable "Hindenburg Line."

To remark upon the enthusiasm with which the Battalion as a whole welcomed the decision, might seem superfluous. It was perhaps in the transport lines where it was hailed with the wildest delight. The joy of the drivers knew no bounds.

The horses attached to our transport had, by order of the 11th Brigade Authorities, been taken away and in their stead had been left some very sorry representatives of the equine species.

None but those who witnessed the parting of the drivers with their faithful companions could realise the anguish that surrounded those pathetic farewells. Our horses were considered the best in the Brigade, and every driver was justly proud of his team. In most instances they had been together since the inception of the Battalion Transport. Tears welled up in the eyes of the drivers as they said good-bye to their dumb comrades. It was difficult to keep the drivers interested in their work until the morning of the 28th September, when their horses returned to them, and though the condition of the animals was very much poorer than when taken away, each horse became the recipient of an ovation, greater than which no Melbourne Cup winner has ever been accorded.

SIR JOHN MONASH'S COMMENTS ON THE SITUATION

It will now be interesting to quote our Corps Commander, the late General Sir John Monash, who comments upon the situation in his book "Australian Victories in France," as follows:—

"I have mentioned that early in 1918 all Brigades of the Imperial Service had, owing to declining manpower been reduced from four to three Battalions. In this reduction the Australian Brigades participated only to a small extent.

"Every one of the Australian Battalions had created great traditions. Regimental esprit and pride of unit were very strong. The private soldier valued his Battalion colour patches almost more than any other decoration.

"My predecessor in the Corps Command had directed the abandonment of one Battalion in each, the 9th, 12th and 13th Brigades. The residue of the disbanded Battalions were used to replenish the remaining three Battalions. It was doubtless a measure directed by necessity . . . the flow of reinforcements was steadily diminishing.

"I became fully alive to the difficulties which would present themselves when the fate of still other Battalions would have to be decided. It was a day I wanted to stave off until the last possible moment . .

"Towards the middle of September, 1918, the successful course of the fighting and the moderate rate of wastage had convinced me there was every hope that the strength of the remaining Battalions could be maintained at a useful standard to the end of the campaigning season of that year.

"I felt assured that the disbandment of a number of additional Battalions would seriously impair the fighting spirit of the whole Australian Corps.

"I was prepared to take the chance of being able to carry on until the end of 1918 with all the remaining Battalions intact.

"But I was not permitted to do so. At various times from June to August, an unimaginative department kept harassing me with enquiries . . . . These enquiries were at first ignored, but early in September the Adjutant-General became insistant for a reply . . . . I urged a postponement of the question . . . Looking back, it seems scarcely credible these representations should have been ignored. I procrastinated . . . The responsible authorities overruled my objections, and on September 19th, I received peremptory instructions to disband eight additional Battalions.

"I had no option but to comply. I called my Divisional Commanders together, and with them, decided which Battalions should suffer extinction. . . . It created a situation of extreme difficulty . . . . The whole of the personnel affected raised a very subordinate, but none the less determined, protest.

"One Battalion after another very respectfully, but very firmly, took the stand that they did not wish to disband, but would prefer not to fight as dismembered and scattered portions of other Battalions.

"This attitude, perhaps, bordered on insubordination, but it was conceived for a very worthy purpose. It was a pathetic effort and elicited much sympathy from the senior officers and myself. On the eve of the great operation for the overthrow of the Hindenburg Line, I found myself threatened with the possibilities of internal disaffection.

"This, to outsiders, who could have no understanding of the situation, might impair the fair name and prestige of the Australian Army Corps.

"Up to this stage, the Fourth Army Commander had been in no way concerned in the matter. The pressure came from the War Office and the Adjutant-General's Department.

"Lord Rawlinson's interests, however, now became vitally involved. . . . I pointed out to him how inopportune was the time for risking trouble of this nature. The order for disbandment having been given, must stand and obedience must be insisted upon, but a postponement of further action for fourteen days was desirable . . . .

"Rawlinson accepted my views in their entirety, and used his authority and influence with the Commander-in-Chief.

"A postponement of action was authorised and all Battalions which had been threatened with extinction, with one exception, were to remain intact during the remainder of the fighting period."

It is needless to state that at the time we performed our "remonstrance" we had not the slightest idea that such sympathy towards us existed in the minds of our superior officers.

Pride

Last Battle—The Capture of the Hindenburg Line

The Assault of the Hindenburg Line

It was intended that two Divisions of U.S.A. troops should attack and capture the Hindenburg Line at certain points, between Le Catelet and Bellicourt, where the Somme-Escaut Canal runs underground through a tunnel.

Whilst this operation was being performed under the protection of a barrage, two Australian Divisions, namely, the 3rd and the 5th, were to leap-frog through the Americans and carry on the advance. At 8 o'clock on the night of September 27th, we moved out from Doingt. Owing to the great congestion of traffic our progress was slow, and this was accentuated by intense darkness. Our bivouac in consequence was not reached until midnight.

The route taken was along the Peronne—Roisel Road to Roisel, thence to Beau Lecois, and onwards in an easterly direction. We found the area to be absolutely devoid of shelter of any description. The weather was cold and frosty, in consequence of which we spent a cold uncomfortable night and did not sleep particularly well.

The next day we took advantage of the shelter afforded by a huge shell-crater. Whilst waiting there enemy artillery became very active, and hostile aircraft paid us assiduous attention by dropping bombs in our neighbourhood.

NON-SUCCESS OF THE AMERICAN TROOPS

On September 29th at 5.40 a.m. two Divisions of American troops attacked the Hindenburg Line between Bellicourt and Bony. A heavy artillery barrage was provided for them, but unfortunately they lost direction, and worse than that, neglected to "mop-up" the defences of the enemy over which they passed.

The attack was unsuccessful and the objectives were

not reached. Owing to this failure, Australian troops which should have been engaged in exploiting the expected success, were unable to reach even their jumping-off line. Instead, they were hastily sent forward to force the Hindenburg Line, which as stated before, should have been already accomplished.

Our zero time was 6.45 a.m. The barrage was an exceedingly good one. At this time our observation balloons moved forward 3,000 yards. We advanced in column, with fifty yards interval between platoons and later went on in artillery formation. We had only with us A, B, and D. Companies, our C Company having been split up into working parties and other details.

Besides heavy shelling and machine-gun fire, which was expected, we encountered a strong concentration of tear-gas, which however, cleared off within an hour.

When the leading Battalions of the Brigade topped the ridge, they discovered themselves to be in the midst of heavy machine-gun fire from the direction of Gillemont Farm and Malakoff Wood. Field-guns were also firing from the support line of the Hindenburg Line.

The severe losses sustained by the American troops were due, partly to their inexperience, but mainly to the fact that in their excitement and enthusiasm, they had rushed forward impetuously, and had passed by the enemy's hiding places. After the Americans had got well forward, the enemy emerged from concealment and shot at the Yanks from the rear.

Australians had long ago learnt their lesson, and never failed to perform the operation called "mopping-up." Had the Americans attended to this most important factor, they would have saved themselves and the Australian troops, the loss of many valuable lives.

THE FORTY-SECOND ENTERS THE HINDENBURG LINE

We had to make good the incomplete work of the Yanks by resorting to the difficult and arduous process of bombing out every likely harbouring place. Through this, the advance of the 11th Brigade to the Hindenburg Line was held up until 3.30 p.m.

Although shelling by the enemy was not heavy at this juncture, it was consistent, and caused us many casualties. A large number of our tanks were put out of action by anti-tank weapons, and so at least were two of our armoured cars which got as far as Bony.

So far as war in the air was concerned, we had absolute mastery. At 4.45 p.m. our companies moved off and again encountered heavy shell-fire as they took up positions near some cross roads. Our B Company proceeded to "mop-up" Malakoff Wood and cleared it of the foe, but fire from enemy machine-guns and shell fire rendered the place a very "hot shop."

Our A Company went through B Company and entered the Hindenburg Line. One platoon proceeded to "mop-up" the front line from south to north, with another platoon in close support, whilst yet another platoon was operating in a similar manner in the support line. We were throwing away no chances.

Immediately upon our approach, enemy troops bolted down into tunnels, and were dealt with. Our A Company continued to work northwards along the Hindenburg Line until they had passed the forward elements of the 44th Battalion, about 300 yards north of the locality called Top Lane.

Meanwhile B Company had taken up a position in Quinnemont Pit Lane from Malakoff Wood to Paul Farm. D Company was in reserve, for several hours after dark, under some low banks, and they were experiencing a pretty miserable existence. Besides numberless machine-gun bullets flying around unceasingly, storms of heavy rain made matters still more uncomfortable. Eventually D Company was withdrawn to a trench which gave some slight measure of shelter.

All this time shelling in this area was heavy and consistent. The enemy placed his machine-guns in cleverly-concealed positions, within extremely short range, and made determined attempts to push us back by vigorously attacking with bombs.

We hung on with grim determination, but the thinness of our ranks, the weather conditions, and the lack of hot food, all conspired to make the task one of extreme difficulty. Still we persevered, and held the position until next day, September 30th, in spite of many untoward incidents. The splendid work of the runners might here be mentioned. It was a task, intricate and hazardous in the extreme for them to negotiate the immense masses of barbed wire entanglements which spread in all directions, and the enshrouding darkness rendered the surroundings an almost inpenetrable maze. Under such circumstances, it was not to be wondered that messages should have been slightly delayed.

At one time there was a most unsatisfactory congestion of troops. It happened when the trenches were packed with Americans and 42nd men. On the arrival of the 43rd, 33rd, and 35th Battalions, in the vicinity of Top Lane to Malakoff Wood Gully, there was such a dense accumulation of troops that it was decided the 35th Battalion should withdraw until such time as the front line troops advanced and made room for the others.

Throughout the day our A Company was in touch with the enemy. Bombing encounters took place continuously though no appreciable amount of ground was gained. Their trenches were commanded by at least six enemy machine-guns, one of which could not be located, although it was only fifty yards away. It was very skilfully hidden in a mass of barbed-wire, but subsequently it was brilliantly knocked out by one of A Company's N.C.O.'s.

Tanks at this time were still unsuccessful. Several were put out of action by shell-fire from the direction of Bony. The others were withdrawn.

It appears that our A Company was responsible for most of the activity against the enemy on this day, September 30th, and it was seen to that they were kept well supplied with ammunition and bombs. At 6 p.m. we were ordered to "hold fast," and pin-point the line in anticipation of the taking of the tunnel by the 9th and 10th Brigades.

At midnight orders were received to relieve the 44th Battalion which we started to do forthwith, but the operation was rendered exceedingly difficult on account of the intense darkness, rain, and the slippery state of the ground. Thick uncut wire entanglements were encountered in all directions, so that we were not able to carry out the completion of the relief until 4 a.m. on October 1st. Although we were utterly weary and out of sorts there still existed the will and determination to clean up the position which at that time was far from satisfactory.

We evenually took up positions as follows:—D Company in the front line, B Company along the Canal Tunnel, commanding the entrance, with A Company in support. D Company was in touch with the 5th Australian Division on the right and with the 43rd Battalion on the left. Among our captures were a high velocity 10 centimetre gun, 4 '77 guns, and about 150 machine-guns.

The 10th Brigade made good progress in the Tunnel, and at 6 p.m. their line extended to The Knob, Bony Point.

The 33rd Battalion, which was attached to the 11th Brigade, pushed through us and held on from Bony Point.

From daylight till evening Battalion Intelligence Section did splendid observation work, and reported many good targets for the direction of our fire.

Communication to companies was maintained by lamp and runner to Command Post, thence touch was preserved direct to Headquarters and Brigade by lamp and wire, and by wire to both Battalions on our flanks.

At noon, Battalion Headquarters were established at Command Post. The difficult and arduous task of keeping the men well supplied with hot meals was carried out by the Battalion Transport, which brought the meals up to the front line on pack mules, and though at times they were very much delayed, which caused us to grouse and grumble, it was realised, later on, how well and capably the transport had carried out its duties.

At 11 o'clock p.m. D Company was advised that the enemy was thought to be clearing out from Le Catelet. Patrols were immediately sent out to get in touch with the enemy. Machine-gun fire was encountered from the direction of Le Catelet and Guoy, whilst salvoes of shells came over from an easterly direction.

The next day, October 2nd, found us still "hanging on" and carrying out some very active patrolling work. The night had been clear and starry, but intensely cold. Though we were quite unaware of the fact, this was positively our last night of actual warfare.

Eventually we were relieved by the King's Royal Rifles. They had a trench strength of four Companies of 100 men, whilst all that remained of the 42nd, to be relieved, were three companies of but small numerical strength.

D Company had pushed out a platoon to garrison Le Catelet which was duly relieved, as were B Company in the Tunnel Headquarters, and the other companies.

We moved out in drizzling rain to bivouac for the night, making the best we could of the little shelter that was available. The next day, which was October 3rd, the weather took a decided turn for the better. It was a typical Autumn day. After breakfasting, we took tally of our numbers and discovered that for the last two days our casualties had been remarkably few, but though the final casualty list was light, unfortunately several of our comrades died later from the result of wounds and sickness.

We eventually set out for Driencourt, where a hot meal awaited our arrival. There was no lack of accommodation in tin shelters and dugouts. Resting there for one day, we departed on the morning of October 5th. The weather was particularly fine as we marched along to Aizecourt-le-Haut, whence we were taken by light railway to Peronne. Here we changed into a train which took us back over the territory we had so recently captured; past many well-remembered places, to which the civilians were gradually returning; past war-scarred Villers-Bretonneux, thence on to Amiens, that picturesque and important town which was saved by the Third Division from falling into the hands of the enemy. At 7 o'clock that night the train drew into the station at Arraines. From here we marched ten kilometres to the pleasant little village of Vergies, and at one hour before midnight, were all snugly billeted. In less time than it takes to tell, we were tucked up in our blankets, sleeping the most peaceful sleep we had known for many a month.

Our travelling cookers and mess-cart arrived next day, having travelled by transport train.

OUR FIGHTING DAYS ARE OVER

Although the Armistice was not signed until about six weeks later, our work as a fighting unit of the Australian Imperial Forces had ended. At this juncture, however, we were not aware of that fact, but what we were quite certain of, beyond the shadow of a doubt, was

A TYPICAL CONCRETE FIRE STEP, HINDENBURG LINE, SEPTEMBER, 1918.

that the Imperial High Command continued as determined and relentless as ever to accomplish something we had defied the enemy to do, namely, smash the 42nd Battalion.

THE THIRD ATTEMPT TO BREAK UP THE FORTY-SECOND

On October 10th, the Battalion paraded and, according to expectations, we were again addressed by our Commanding Officer.

He once more emphasised the necessity for the disbandment of the Battalion and urged the men to gravely consider the result of their actions and advised them to obey orders.

There were some few men who had expressed a desire to be transferred to other units, and these stepped aside when their names were called. The remainder stood firm, and when the command to "March" was given there was not a movement from one of them.

After this third resistance on our part, ceremonial parades, route marches, and general training occupied our days, excepting on the Sunday, when we attended a Church parade.

And so the fate of the Battalion still hung in the balance.

THE FOURTH, AND FINAL EFFORT TO EXTINGUISH THE BATTALION

The final effort to break up the Battalion was made on October 14th, on which occasion, when we paraded, our Commanding Officer was accompanied by Staff-officers from the 3rd Divisional Headquarters and the 11th Brigade, and these officers included the General Officer Commanding the Division, General Gellibrand.

The men were cautioned against disobedience to orders. One of the senior officers then read "The Riot Act," after which the order to "March" was given. And again, not one man moved. All officers then left the parade ground. We were taken for a route march, and upon our return it was discovered that our Cookers had been taken away.

We were informed that the 42nd no longer existed, and that henceforward we were to be designated "The 11th Brigade Training Battalion."

But the pathetic struggle to "stick together" continued. A more subtle plan was therefore devised to expedite the dismemberment. During the next few days many N.C.O.'s and other aspirants for promotion were drafted to training schools. Any man complaining of the slightest ailment was forthwith sent to hospital, whilst leave to Paris or England, was freely granted.

By such means were the ranks of the 42nd so depleted that whatever resistance might have been offered, could be but feeble.

Upon our arrival at Vergies the strength of the Battalion was 35 officers and 500 other ranks. All that now remained was but 273 all told. This remnant, along with the Brass and Pipe Bands, was transferred, intact, to the 41st Battalion, and henceonwards, until demobilisation, was known as "B Company of the 41st."

Thus, we were still a distinct body. A unit, within a unit, with which it never merged.

And so, was sacrificed the 42nd Battalion.

From the ashes of that sacrifice arose the unmistakable signs of its unquellable spirit.

* * * * * *

It is with feelings of deepest pride that we leave to posterity the traditions of our Glorious Battalion, the annals of its devotion to duty and its sacrifices, but above all, we bequeath the Inspiration of its Spirit. The Spirit which encouraged us in the hours of danger and hardship; the Spirit which united its members in harmony and mutual trust, and which twenty years later, proudly survives, and will, we venture to predict, endure so long as there be but two 42nd men left to stick together.

Comradeship

Demobilisation—Return to Australia

The History of B Company of the Forty-First

It may now be of interest to learn what befell the 42nd Battalion in its new guise as B Company of the 41st, and of the subsequent return to Queensland of that large number of 42nd men who formed part of what was known as "The 39th Quota" of which our own Commanding Officer, Lt-Colonel A. R. Woolcock was in command.

WE LEAVE VERGIES FOR WARLUS

It was on October 21st, that we marched from Vergies to take up our new position with the 41st Battalion.

We were duly inspected by our new Commanding Officer on the 25th, when we undertook our first route march along with the 41st Battalion. We still wore our 42nd colour patches, and continued to do so in spite of all orders to the contrary.

We carried on daily with training and were plagued with what were termed "Ceremonial Parades," included in which was a stunt which we dubbed "The Prussian Mad Mile." The term is self-explanatory. And then we had all the paraphernalia of the "bull-ring," which was a continuous performance, lasting over a couple of hours, during which time we were put through physical exercises, bayonet fighting, bomb-throwing, marching, jumping; in fact, all the arts of the bull and the toreador put together.

There were also competitions for shooting, which took place at the rifle range near by.

Having during the past months of continuous activity, slipped somewhat from the path of cleanliness, we rejoiced at the prospect of renewing our acquaintance with the art of keeping clean, and embraced every opportunity that was afforded to bathe in good baths that had been established in a village called Allory.

Our favourite haunt at night was Arraines, where estaminets and egg-and-chip warehouses did a flourishing trade.

THE ARMISTICE

Whilst we were at Warlus the most important event of the War occurred. On November 11th, we learnt that the Armistice had been signed. Immediately thoughts passed through our minds of the problems that faced us with regard to earning our future livelihood.

Military training was relaxed forthwith, and in its place, educational schemes were put forward and efforts to assist us to again take our places in civilian life were made.

It was on November 26th, 1916, that the 42nd landed in France, so when that anniversary came round again in 1918 we decided the event was one worthy of being celebrated. This we accordingly did, and with gusto.

Early in December we moved out from Warlus and took up our abode at a village called St. Maxent, twelve kilometres distant from Abbeville. But though we changed our residence our daily routine was unaltered. Adjacent to ours, were several interesting villages each with a quaintness particularly its own. The principal of them all was called Oisement, which might be designated a town, for it had a large market-place and on market days, presented a very animated scene. Leave to Amiens and Abbeville was easily attainable, and it was less difficult now to obtain leave to England and Paris.

Christmas 1918 was spent under very different conditions to those of the two previous years. We had a splendid Christmas dinner. A cheque for £100, received from the 42nd Battalion Comforts Fund, organised by Queensland ladies, was the means of making the festive season more festive than ever.

New Years Day was celebrated the following week, and probably as a New Year's gesture of goodwill, the military authorities performed a good deed a few days later. They lightened our load considerably. Henceforward we were to march in "Fighting Order," which meant our old bug-bear, the pack, had been discarded for good.

NON-MILITARY EMPLOYMENT

Non-military employment was a scheme put forward with a view to help the placing of men in employment upon demobilisation. Firms in Great Britain offered opportunities to us to learn trades, whilst schools, academies and institutes were made available to others wishing to follow up a profession.

Many availed themselves of these offers, and eagerly filled in the necessary form. In due course they were sent to Blighty and for the time being, became practically "soldier-civilians."

The scheme seemed a good one to us, and those who availed themselves of it were called "schemers," and instead of "Non-Military Employment," it was referred to as "Bon Military Enjoyment."

ST. MAXENT

For those who did not take advantage of the scheme, the daily routine at St. Maxent was relaxed. The exercise that was insisted upon was just sufficient to keep us healthy.

The months that passed whilst awaiting demobilisation were made as pleasant for us as circumstances would permit.

Now, as the time grew nearer when we should again be civilians and move among our dearest ones, it was not unnatural that many found their thoughts turning towards the more devotional side of life. This was indicated by the increasing attendances at Church parades of all denominations.

DANCING

Many were the methods introduced to make the time of waiting less wearisome. Without doubt, the most successful of them all was the pastime of dancing. The proposal, on being tried out, immediately caught on. So popular did it prove, that many who prior to the War had never attempted to dance a step, were now found among the most proficient and enthusiastic exponents of the art. It was astonishing to witness the manner in which men danced together in their great, heavy, sprigged-soled, leather Cossacks.

OUR PARTNERS

After a while, dancing with male partners lost its charm, so we invited seventy-five Waacs to a special dance. These Waacs were members of the Women's Army Auxiliary Corps, the initials of which go to make up the name by which they were always known to us. They were transported to and from our camp by motor-lorries.

The success that attended this experimental dance was so great that several others were subsequently arranged, as were also sports gatherings where both Diggers and Waacs entered into competition. We also had some fights with these Waacs, but only snow-fights, and these were greatly enjoyed. The Waacs usually got the better of us in these encounters being more used to snow games, whereas few Australians had ever seen snow prior to arriving in these regions.

THE Y.M.C.A. MARQUEE AND HUTS.

The floor of the Marquee where the dancing took place was laid down by the Diggers. The Marquee itself was erected by the Young Men's Christian Association, or as it was termed by the men—"The Y. Emma C. Ack!" There were also provided for us, the use of four large Nissen Huts, wherein were facilities for reading, writing, and for the playing of games such as draughts, chess and billiards. A piano, gramophones, a fair library and files of Australian and English newspapers and magazines were at our disposal.

Our baths had been removed to a place called Huppy. The frequent use we made of these baths helped to keep the men fit, and the chats away.

EXHIBITION OF ARTS AND CRAFTS

During February, an exhibition of Australian Arts and Crafts was opened at a place called Martainville. The exhibitors were all of them members of the Third Division, and many beautiful and artistic specimens were among the objects of handicraft displayed.

There were also boxing tournaments and other contests, whilst the Divisional Concert Party, "The Coo-ees" entertained with songs and jokes. The Y.M.C.A. established a canteen to cater for the inner man. Altogether, it was a splendidly organised show, greatly appreciated by one and all as a wonderful break in the dull monotony of waiting.

YEARNING FOR AUSTRALIA

Our thoughts were for ever turning in the direction of Australia. Now that our job was done, none of us could get home quickly enough. There was, unfortunately, at this time, an industrial upheaval in England, which made it appear to us, who were so eager to get home, that we were doomed to be exiled in France for an interminable period. Scathing was the criticism levelled at the tactics of those who were responsible for delaying our return.

It was not before the middle of February that our first quota for home was formed. Everyone seemed to want to get out on the "first wave." A little excitement was now added to the monotonous daily routine, by the inauguration of kit inspections, medical examinations, and medical boards.

OOZE, SLUSH AND MUD

And now the snow began to melt. The rain began to fall. The ice began to thaw. The French villages where we lived or frequented became the very acme of discomfort and dreariness. We designated our village "Venice on the Mud," and the young French girls we called "Muddy-moiselles." The ground was sodden. The roads oozed with mud and slush. Even the main highway was in an appalling condition, but we had put up with a great deal worse than that at Passchendaele.

Our first quota eventually left St. Maxent, on March 18th. Two nights prior to this, a dance was held to mark the occasion, to which were invited the mademoiselles of the village of St. Maxent.

Our departing comrades were accorded a rousing farewell, as they left for a town called Gamaches, en route for England and Australia.

WHILING AWAY THE TIME

We now settled down to get over the period which had to elapse before our second quota of "homing birds" would make ready to fly. A series of interesting lectures was instituted. The subjects selected give a bearing on the trend of thought at that time. They were: Unionism, Strikes, Women in Industry, Bolshevism, and Problems facing Australia.

The appeal of the dance continued. We had another party to which we invited the mademoiselles of Doodlenville, and then to vary things a little, a few nights later, invitations were issued to another batch of Waacs.

The 11th Brigade Concert Party, "The Blue-gums," came along to help us while away the time. They presented a really first-class concert, to a large audience in which were included many French people who appeared to enjoy the presentation in spite of the fact that they could not understand our language.

Another visitation of heavy falls of snow arrived, accompanied by gusts of piercing wind. Then rain turned up in full force and succeeded in mixing up the snow with mud, so that wherever the eye rested only thick, filthy slush was discernable.

THE BEGINNING OF A NEW SERIES OF MEDICAL EXAMINATIONS

Although it needed but one medical examination to pass one into the army, it was obvious that innumerable medical inspections would be necessary before one could be discharged. We had completely lost count of all the inspections we had undergone in the past, but now we started off scratch and began all over again in real earnest. The first of the "new series" took place on April 9th.

A MOVE NEARER HOME

About the middle of April we progressed a little towards Australia. We bid farewell to St. Maxent and moved to the town of Gamaches, which although only a few kilometres distant, was the recognised starting-off point for Home. Whilst here we underwent a medical examination.

CHINESE LABOUR TROOPS

There were a great number of Chinese coolies employed in this locality, engaged in all kinds of laborious jobs. They were segregated in compounds. During the course of the War they had been utilised in carrying out much useful work in the back areas. Few, if any, of us could understand their language, but they all seemed happy enough in spite of that drawback.

They too, had their concert party. Some of us attended a performance of a Chinese pierrot show. Being unable to form the least conception of their entertainment, it appeared somewhat ridiculous to us. Their singing was awful.

LE HAVRE

At length, on April 23rd, we left Gamaches by troop train. This train was composed entirely of German trucks which had been captured. We found them rather more comfortable than those of the French Railways. Each truck was equipped with a stove, which enabled us to make hot tea and cocoa for our midday meal.

We duly arrived at Le Havre at 11 o'clock that night.

WE SHED OUR FIGHTING EQUIPMENT

The following day was one of the utmost importance. It was a day of parting, but there was no trace of a tear in any eye as we said "Good-bye" to our webbing equipment, and packs. This was handed over, along with rifles and steel helmets, to German prisoners of War, who were employed at the store at Le Havre. Thus standing, relieved of every accoutrement of warfare, even to the box-respirator, with only our uniforms to suggest that we were once soldiers, we began to imagine that we had been transformed straight away into civilians. But the feeling was only momentary. Another medical inspection was at hand to remind us we were still in the army.

ANZAC DAY 1919

We celebrated Anzac Day whilst at Le Havre.

A monster sports gathering was presented. Soldiers of any of the Allied Forces were permitted to participate in any of the events. Some French naval men engaged our boys in a tug-o'-war, but were not quite good enough. Our girl friends, the Waacs, entered keenly into many of the races and competitions.

ADIEU TO FRANCE

During the next few days it rained, which was very depressing, but we cheered up when on Monday, April

28th, we bid Adieu to France. It was an agreeable surprise when we found that we were to be transported to the wharf by motor-lorries. Such transport was unusual for infantry. It was generally understood that everywhere the infantryman went, he must walk. This was indeed a change.

In the evening we embarked on the s.s. "St. David," and after quite a good passage across the English Channel, disembarked the following morning at Southampton and entrained for Codford, a town on Salisbury Plain.

CODFORD

Soon after arrival we were medically examined and innoculated against influenza, which was raging. Here at Codford, we found ourselves, for the first time in our experience, living in a camp that was near to a railway station. The town, too, was unexpectedly handy.

It was that type of town generally found near to military camps. Along the main street were canteens, branches of most of the principal banks, and temporary stores where it was possible to purchase every requirement at a reasonable figure, provided one did not wear the Australian uniform, which was the signal for popping up the prices.

The period was the middle of spring. The surrounding country was to be seen under the most pleasant conditions. Wherever the eye rested, a picture awaited its gaze. Beautiful landscapes, trees and hedges of verdant green, wild flowers of every hue, fruit trees a blaze of bloom, and all kinds of plant life in leaf and bud.

THE THIRTY-NINTH QUOTA

We now became members of the thirty-ninth quota, and on May 22nd, our names were checked on the boat-roll.

The occasion was celebrated by again calling upon us to undergo a medical examination. But what did we care? It was another step nearer Home, and we had become quite resigned and impervious to medical inspections, yet we did have a surprise when on June 5th, as a final souvenir from the English doctors, we were again stabbed with the needle, as a further precaution against influenza. Next day, we had "a medical examination."

Early on June 12th, we vacated Codford Camp, and realised that we had at last really started on our journey to Australia.

After a pleasant journey by train we eventually reached Devonport, embarked upon the tender which took us out to our transport, the s.s. "Thermistocles."

ABOARD THE TRANSPORT

Anchor was weighed on FRIDAY, the THIRTEENTH of June. It was said that a black cat had fallen overboard and was drowned.

One of our fellows stated he had seen a clairvoyant, when on leave, who foretold that he would never reach Australia without mishap.

The officer in charge of troops was our own C.O. Lt.-Colonel A. R. Woolcock. The adjutant was another 42nd Battalion officer.

We were fortunate in having with us two concert parties, namely, "The Coo-ees," and the Third Machine Gunners Concert Party, called "The Apres-la-Guerres." We also had a good band and an orchestra.

Other means of recreation were afforded in the way of lectures, debates and talks illustrated by lantern slides.

Mention of the padre who was with us must not be omitted. He was a ball of energy, and his interest in the welfare of the troops never flagged for a moment. Due to his efforts there were all kinds of stunts and competitions for our amusement and entertainment. For the more serious aspect of catering for the needs of our future employment, no less than twenty-five distinct classes of vocational training were inaugurated and well attended.

During the voyage we received news that Germany had signed the Peace Treaty at Versailles.

Eventually we arrived at Cape Town. Here we found the citizens bent upon giving the visiting Australian troops as good a time as possible. So well did they succeed in their endeavours that each man must have carried away with him lasting impressions of an unselfish, hospitable, and loving people. We were received into private homes, taken for pleasure trips, and invited to teas, tennis afternoons, and musical evenings.

We remained in Cape Town for two days, embarked

again on the night of July 2nd, and resumed the voyage on July 3rd, in good weather. We all of us thought our next stop would be Melbourne, and little thought that in two days time we should be back again in Cape Town under sad and distressing circumstances.

COLLISION AT SEA

It was a quarter of an hour before midnight on July 3rd, in the midst of a dense fog, that our transport came into collision with another vessel, the "Edderside," a Norwegian barque, bound from Durban to Buenos Ayres with a full cargo of coal.

At the time of striking, the troops were in their hammocks, most of them fast asleep. The noise of the impact was awful. Everyone awakened with a start. Some were thrown from their hammocks. The Alarm was sounded. Everyone was summoned on deck and ordered to "Stand to Boat-stations."

Life-belts were donned. All were filled with expectancy as they made themselves ready for the emergency of leaving the ship by boat or raft. Happily we were not called upon to take the midnight plunge.

The Transport stopped immediately the crash was heard. The sea could not be discerned from the decks owing to the dense fog. Several minutes elapsed broken only by the shrieking of the Transport's syren. Cries of distress came to our ears. Meanwhile the ship's boats had been lowered. In them were rescuers with lighted flares. The calls for "Help" were heart-rending. The fog made the task of rescue difficult and arduous.

Survivors clung to the wreckage of the "Edderside," which sank within five minutes of the collision. Eventually "thirteen" of the unfortunate crew were brought on board. It was understood that eight or more had perished.

We remained in the vicinity of the disaster until long after daybreak, when careful search failed to reveal any more survivors. Reluctantly leaving the scene we headed for Cape Town.

It was evident that the Transport had sustained much damage. A collection for the shipwrecked men was taken up among the troops resulting in the amount of £160 being subscribed, which was largely augmented by the

ST. MAXENT, 1919.
A Battle in the snow (Apres la Guerre).

series of benefit concerts given in Cape Town by "The Coo-ees."

So, within forty-eight hours of leaving Cape Town, we were back again, with even the least superstitious among us, fully convinced that Friday is a bad day to leave port, and THIRTEEN is indeed an ominous number.

BEHAVIOUR OF TROOPS IN ACCORDANCE WITH BRITISH TRADITIONS

The Cape Town "Argus," on July 10th, 1919, published the findings of the Court of Enquiry that was appointed, among which was the following comment:—

> "It is very pleasing and gratifying to learn that the 1,500 Australian troops behaved most splendidly, in accordance with the traditions of the British race, and the Court is thankful to the Almighty that a second Birkenhead disaster did not occur."

The people of Cape Town made, if possible, a greater fuss of us than they did before, evidently regarding us, more or less, as shipwrecked heroes. We consequently got quite used to the place and found ourselves treated more like residents than enforced visitors.

The "Themistocles" was ordered to Simonstown for docking and repairs, and on July 8th, we re-embarked, and next morning floated into the fine up-to-date dry-dock at Simonstown. The damage to the "Themistocles" consisted of three broken propeller blades and a bent tail-shaft. The ship was compelled to remain in "hospital" for several days.

This necessitated the withdrawal of all troops from the Transport. We were thereupon ordered, some into military barracks at Simonstown, and the rest into an Imperial Garrison Camp at Wynburg, a suburb of Cape Town.

After a week of sightseeing and entertainment, we returned to the "Themistocles" at Simonstown, and on Sunday, July 20th (not Friday, this time) set sail for Australia.

FUN AND FROLIC AT SEA

We were at sea on August 4th, the anniversary of the outbreak of hostilities, so it was decided to commemorate it with celebrations on a large scale.

Humour was the dominant note in the day's proceedings, which started with a fancy dress carnival. There were over one hundred entrants in this competition for the most original personation, and many of them were well thought out and sustained. The winner represented "an Influenza Patient," whilst the second prize went to "A Demobilised Digger and His English Bride."

A "Telegraph Messenger" delivered supposed wireless messages to various well-known persons on board, causing much laughter at the expense of the recipients.

Busking parties, imitating street-singers, went the rounds of the decks, and the days entertainment was brought to a close by the holding of a Mock Court of (in)-Justice.

Port Phillip Heads were eventually reached on Friday, August 5th.

ANOTHER MEDICAL INSPECTION

Before the ship berthed at Port Melbourne, we had to undergo another medical examination, and then, as the bands on board played "Home, Sweet Home," and "Should Auld Acquaintance be Forgot," we parted with our comrades from Western Australia, South Australia and Victoria. The remainder, who were Queenslanders and New South Welshmen, were granted leave for the afternoon, and it was not long before we had the pleasure of promenading the streets of an Australian city, after an absence of over three years.

We resumed our voyage the following day, reaching Sydney on Monday, August 11th. This port was the destination of the "Themistocles." We disembarked and were taken from Wooloomooloo, through the streets of Sydney, in private motor cars, which conveyed us to the special train awaiting to take us back to our beloved Sunny Queensland.

APPRECIATION OF LADY WAR-WORKERS, NURSES, AND V.A.D.'s

The New South Wales people treated us splendidly, entertaining us at Gosford with a dinner, and further on, at Werris Creek, we received still more refreshments.

We changed trains at Wallangarra, where Queensland friends provided us with breakfast. All along the line there were manifestations of pleasure at our return. Stanthorpe, Warwick, Toowoomba, Helidon, Ipswich vied with each other in offering their hospitality. As for our lady war-workers, nurses, and V.A.D.'s, they can never be forgotten whilst any 42nd man lives.

This narrative is a fitting place where appreciation of the self-sacrificing work performed on our behalf can be recorded.

We eventually arrived in Brisbane, and before many hours had passed, received our discharges, after having undergone another medical inspection.

The War was over. Our term of service was completed.

MEMORIES

All that remain are "Memories." Glorious Memories! Memories that insist there is something grand and noble in the friendship established between man and man; in the friendship that was born in camp and cemented on the fields of battle, midst fire, danger and hardship.

For thus it was that the men of the Forty-second Battalion, A.I.F., became welded into a band of faithful comrades.

* * * * * *

It is hoped this narrative may provide a further impetus towards fanning "The Flame of Remembrance," and cause those now living, and generations to come, to realise the depth and significance of

"THE SPIRIT OF THE FORTY-SECOND."

The End.

BATTALION OFFICERS AT LOCRE, FEBRUARY, 1918.

Roll of Officers who Returned.

•

LIEUT.-COLONELS:
WOOLCOCK, Arthur Raff, D.S.O., C. de G., M.I.D.
FARRELL, John, D.S.O., M.I.D.
HERON, Alexander Robert, C.M.G., D.S.O., M.I.D.

MAJORS:
CAMPBELL, Colin Clyde, M.B.E.
DIBDIN, Edward John, D.S.O., M.I.D.
HARDIE, John, M.C.
  (Attached A.A.M.C.)
MOYES, Aubrey Clyde, M.C.
WOOD, Thomas Patrick
  (Chaplain Attached)

CAPTAINS:
ANDERSON, Leslie William Charles
BINNIE, David Johnstone
BURDEN, Alexander Cleghorn Mitchell
CAMERON, Gavin Holmes
  (Attached A.A.M.C.)
CAMERON, Colin Ralph
DUNBAR, Gordon Allen, C. de G., M.C., M.I.D.
FAITHFULL, Geoffrey Mervyn
  (Attached A.A.M.C.)
FINLAY, John
JONES, H. W. *(Chaplain)*
LEAHY, John, M.I.D.
MILLS, Thomas
O'BRYEN, Richard de Burgh Falkiner, M.I.D.
PICKERING, Richard Fleetwood, M.C.
POTT, Arthur
RANKIN, Robert Stuart
ST. JOHN, Arthur Percival, M.C.
THOMSON, Ewing George, M.C.
  (Attached A.A.M.C.)
WARRY, Stanley Richard, M.C.
YELLAND, Ernest, M.I.D.

LIEUTENANTS:
ALBREY, John Richard
ALLEN, William Ewart, M.C.
ARMSTRONG, George Douglas
ARMSTRONG, Herbert James
BARNES, Leslie Walter, M.C.
BAXTER, Angus McDonald
BEAMISH, Thomas Renney
BEATTY, Alfred Joseph
BOORMAN, Arthur Charles, M.C.
BROADFOOT, Cecil James
BROOM, Colin Vincent McIntosh
BULL, Henry William McKell
BYRNE, Francis Hilary
BYRNE, William James
CLACHER, Thomas Frederick
CRAIL, Herbert
DAVIDSON, Charles William
DENT, Sydney Harold
DINNIE, Robert Davidson
DIBDIN, Arthur Coleman
DIXON, Victor Charles, D.C.M.
FISHER, Robert David, M.C.
FORSTER, George Beverley, M.M. and Bar.
FRANCIS, Vincent
FRANKHAM, George, M.M., M.I.D.
FRASER, Donald Lovat
GERMEIN, Walter Clifford
GILMOUR, Hugh Edmond, M.M.
HAGGETT, Walter Charles, M.M.
HAMILTON, Hugh John
HANLON, Grant Clinton
HARLEY, Leslie
HORSBOROUGH, Arthur Bland
HOSKINS, Edwin Darlston
HULL, Henry Ainsley
JOLLY, Etienne Arnold
JOSEPH, Henry Edgar
KEATING, William Frederick
KEYSOR, Leonard, V.C.

LATIMER, Wallace Edward
LEEDS, Frank Adrian
LEWIS, Thomas Swetenham
LORIARD, Cyril Herrington Grier, M.C.
MOLE, Cyril Bayard
MOON, Edgar
MURDOCH, Kenneth Adrian, M.I.D.
MURRAY, James Alexander
McLEAN, John, D.S.O., M.C., M.I.D.
McLEOD, Scott
NEEDHAM, Francis Jack
NEWMAN, Percival
O'CONNELL, Garnet William Cecil
O'CONNOR, Walter Leonard, M.C., M.M.
PATERSON, Clarence George
PATERSON, Eric Ewan, M.C.
PATTISON, John Grant, M.M.
PENDER, James Stanley
PENMAN, Hugh Taylor Currie
PRICE, James Henry Norman, M.C., M.I.D.

SAVAGE, Percy Henry
SHAW, William Hugh
SHEPHERD, Christopher Thompson Ousby
SLATTER, Francis Leichhardt
SMITH, Horace
SMITH, Leslie Moreton
SNELLING, Arthur Frederick, M.C.
SNOW, Geoffrey William
SQUIRES, Hurtle Abel Roy, M.I.D.
STANLEY, Arthur
STEVENSON, Ernest McKenzie, M.C.
TARDENT, Jules Louis, C. de G.
TEITZEL, Arthur Leslie
TEVLIN, Michael Percy
THOMPSON, Richard Harold
TIERNEY, Thomas Desmond, M.C.
TILLIDGE, Clarence
TRUDGIAN, Clarence Samuel, M.C.
WOOD, Arthur Barclay Chapman
WOOD, John Frederick, M.C.
WRENCH, Robert James

Officers Killed in Action.

•

CAPTAINS:
HALSTEAD, Albert Edward, M.C.
McDONNELL, William Hildig Armstrong, M.C.
JACK, Thomas, M.C.

LIEUTENANTS:
BALLARD, Albert Edward
BARTLEY, Thomas James
BROWNE, Gordon Minto
CARR, Elwyne Albert
COMPER, William Henry
COLLIN, Charles Louis
CONRAD, Harold Victor
FISHER, Walde Gerard
FREEMAN, Norman David
GILCHRIST, William

HARRIS, Phillip Vernon
HART, Morris
HOGG, James Scholes
JAMESON, Charles Chalmers
KELLY-HEALY, James Patrick
LAMSDEN, Albert Wheeler
LEWIS, Frederick George
LYONS, Howard Maitland
MACKAY, James Bruce, M.C.
MAY, Richard William
MEIGH, James
PETERSEN, Hans Victor
SANDFORD, Percy Harold
SESSARAGO, Frederick Harold
SURTEES, William
TAYLOR, Leonard
THOMPSON, Kenneth Sanders
WARWICK, Roland

Nominal Roll of the 42nd Battalion, A.I.F.

•

NON-COMMISSIONED OFFICERS AND OTHER RANKS DISCHARGED

Pte. ADAMS, Allan Bass
Sgt. ADAMS, Archibald Hugh
Pte. ADAMS, Bertram Joseph
„ ADAMS, Robert Tait
„ ADAMS, Thomas Frederick
Cpl. ADDISON, John
Pte. AFFLECK, Thomas
„ AHERN, William
„ AITKEN, Adam, M.M.
„ AKERS, George
„ AKRED, James Harold
„ ALAND, Arthur Richard
„ ALEXANDER, Ernest
„ ALEXANDER, Lovegrove William
Sgt. ALEXANDER, Thomas Henry, C. de G.
Pte. ALEXANDER, William
Sgt. ALEXANDER, William Robert, V.
Pte. ALFORD, Richard Ferris
Cpl. ALGAR, George
Pte. ALGAR, William James
„ ALLAN, Alexander William
„ ALLAN, James
„ ALLEN, John Thomas
„ ALLARDICE, John
L./Cpl. ALNE, Carl
Pte. AMOS, Clifton Percival
„ ANDERSON, George
Cpl. ANDERSON, Albert
Pte. ANDERSON, Henry
„ ANDERSON, Herbert Ernest
„ ANDERSON, Joseph
Cpl. ANDERSON, James Johnstone
Pte. ANDERSON, John William G.
„ ANDERSON, Stuart Douglas F.
„ ANDERSON, Thomas Henry

Pte. ANDREA, Martin Jacob
„ ANDREWS, Edward
Cpl. ANDREWS, Norman, M.M.
Sgt. ANGELL, Edward Walter
Pte. ANGELL, George John
„ ANGELL, William
L./Cpl. APPLEBY, Irwin Keith
Sgt. APPLEBY, William Emanuel
Pte. ARCHER, James
L./Cpl. ARCHIBALD, Eric Lyle
W.O. ARMITAGE, John Wilfred
Pte. ARMSTRONG, Archer
„ ARMSTRONG, Herbert
„ ARMSTRONG, James
„ ARMSTRONG, Percy
„ ARKINSTALL, Arthur
L./Cpl. ARNOLD, Alfred Edgar J.
Pte. ARNOLD, Henry John
„ ARNOTT, Edward Charles
„ ARTHUR, George William
„ ARTHUR, Robert
„ ASCOUGH, Richard
„ ASKEW, Arthur
„ ASTILL, John
„ ATTRIDGE, Frank Herbert, M.M., M.I.D.
L./Cpl. AUSTIN, Edward William
„ AUSTIN, Harvey Percy
Pte. AVERY, Clarence Cecil
„ AYRES, Albert
„ AYRES, William George
„ BACKWELL, Edward
„ BAGGS, William James
„ BAGNALL, William Albert, H.
„ BAILEY, Eric Charles R.
Cpl. BAILLIE, Robert

Pte. BAIN, John Herbert
Sgt. BAKER, Joseph
Pte. BALDOCK, Horace Cecil
 „ BALL, Charles
 „ BALL, William James
Sgt. BANNAH, Albert
Pte. BARBIN, William
L./Cpl. BARNETT, David
Sgt. BARNETT, John, M.M.
L./Cpl. BARR, Daniel
Pte. BARRETT, Alfred George
 „ BARRETT, Arthur Leolin
 „ BARRETT, John Cuthbert
 „ BARRY, John Richard
 „ BARRY, Patrick
L./Cpl. BARTON, George
Pte. BARTON, James Vincent
 „ BARTON, William Edward
 „ BATHE, Eber Ezra
 „ BAVISTER, Edwin
 „ BAXTER, Charles Alexander
 „ BAXTER, James
W.O. BAYNES, John Hennessy M.S.M.
Sgt. BEAN, Frederick Richard
Pte. BEATTIE, Thomas
 „ BEATTIE, William
 „ BECK, Charles William
 „ BEECH, William Thomas
Cpl. BEESTON, Francis Alfred
Pte. BEGGS, William Raymond
 „ BEIRNE, Michael Patrick
 „ BEITZ, William Frederick
Pte. BELCHER, Leslie Robert
 „ BELL, Frederick
 „ BELL, Graham, M.M.
 „ BELL, Harry Stanley
Dvr. BELL, Peter
Cpl. BELL, Reginald Robert, M.M.
Sgt. BELL, Septimus H.
Dvr. BELL, William Richard
Pte. BELLAMY, Albert Vincent
 „ BELLINGHAM, Vincent Dennis
 „ BENGTSSON, Edward Herbert
L./Cpl. BENNETT, Arthur Joseph
Pte. BENNETT, George Robert
Sgt. BENNETT, Isaac Edward
Pte. BENNETT, Thomas
 „ BENNEY, George Burleigh
 „ BENTLEY, Roy, M.M.
Cpl. BERRELL, James Patrick
Pte. BERRY, Ernest Charles
 „ BETTRIDGE, John
 „ BETTS, George Frederick
 „ BEVIS, Alfred

Pte. BEVIS, Harry
 „ BEZANT, Harry John
 „ BIERTON, Ambrose
 „ BIGG, Warrington, A.
 „ BILES, Arthur James
 „ BINNINGTON, John
 „ BINNS, Harry
Sgt. BINNS, William Edward
 „ BINNS, Joseph Henry
 „ BIRKETT, Frederick David, M.M.
L./Cpl. BIRKETT, George Victor
Pte. BLACK, Albert Joseph
 „ BLACK, Frank
 „ BLACK, Herbert Henry
 „ BLAINS, Charles Frederick
 „ BLUM, William James
 „ BLUNT, William Henry
Sgt. BODGER, Herbert Ainsworth
 „ BOGUE, John McAllister
L./Cpl. BOLGER, Bernard James
 „ BOLGER, Patrick Vincent
Pte. BONEHAM, Robert
 „ BONGERS, Arthur Clarke
 „ BONSOR, Charles
 „ BOOTH, Arthur Walter
Sgt. BOOTH, William Charles
Pte. BOOTY, William
 „ BORGEN, William Andreas
Cpl. BORGER, John Henry
Pte. BOTT, George William
 „ BOURKE, Edward
 „ BOURKE, Thomas
 „ BOURKE, John Thomas
 „ BOW, Arthur Robert
L./Cpl. BOWDEN, David
Pte. BOX, Percival Albert
 „ BOYCE, Leslie Fletcher
Cpl. BOYES, Fred
Pte. BOYLE, Francis Frederick
 „ BRADFORD, Charles Henry
Sgt. BRADFORD, Joseph William
Pte. BRADSHAW, Harry William
 „ BRAHMS, Vivian
 „ BRAY, Walter Henry
C.S.M. BREBNER, James, M.I.D.
Pte. BREEN, James Joseph
 „ BREMNER, Leslie Gilbert
 „ BRENNAN, Hugh
 „ BRENNAN, James
 „ BREWER, Edgecombe
Cpl. BREWARD, Albert Leslie
Pte. BREWER, Ralph
 „ BRIDGE, Leonard
 „ BRIDGES, Victor Edwin

N.C.O.'s AND OTHER RANKS DISCHARGED 141

Pte. BRIGGS, Charles
„ BRIGGS, Alfred
L./Cpl. BRIGGS, David
Pte. BRIGGS, Simion
„ BRIGHAM, George Henry
„ BRIGHT, James Frederick, M.M.
„ BRITCHER, William
Sgt. BRITTAIN, William Stanley G.
Pte. BROADHEAD, Horace Augustus
„ BRODIE, Thomas
„ BRODIE, William
„ BROOKS, Ralph Chester
Sgt. BROPHY, Michael James
Pte. BROUGHTON, Ronald Gilbert
„ BROWN, Alfred
Sapper BROWN, Andrew
Pte. BROWN, Edward John
Cpl. BROWN, George Love, M.M. (A.A.M.C.).
Sgt. BROWN, John
Cpl. BROWN, John Sydney
Pte. BROWN, Leopold Russell
„ BROWN, Phillip
„ BROWN, Thomas
„ BROWN, William Henry
Cpl. BROWN, Albert William, M.M.
„ BROWNE, Henry D'Arcy
L./Cpl. BROWNE, Robert James
„ BROWNE, William Michael
Pte. BRUCE, Norman Walter L.
„ BRYANT, Walter James, M.M.
„ BRYCE, Bowie
„ BRYERS, William Joseph
„ BRYSON, William John
Cpl. BUCKINGHAM, Hugh Lachlan
L./Cpl. BUCKLEY, James Frederick
Pte. BUDGEN, John
„ BULCOCK, Leslie John
„ BURGE, Wilfred
„ BURGESS, George Chesworth
„ BURGESS, Richard
„ BURGESS, Thomas
„ BURN, Ralph Lionel
„ BURNETT, Andrew Charles
„ BURNETT, Roy Wallace
„ BURNHAM, Frederick Thompson
„ BURROWS, William Henry
Cpl. BURT, Harry
Pte. BURTON, Robert
„ BUSS, Basil Stockton
„ BUSUTTIN, Basil Charles
L./Cpl. BUTLER, Edmond Francis
Pte. BUTLER, Charles Francis, M.M.
„ BUTTIE, Richard
„ BUTTON, Mark Guy

Pte. BYRNE, Joseph Ambrose
„ CADWALLADER, Richard
„ CAFFERY, John
„ CAFFERY, Edward
„ CAHALAN, Michael Patrick
„ CAHILL, Larry
„ CALLAGHAN, Ernest William
L./Cpl. CAMERON, Andrew
Pte. CAMERON, Allan
„ CAMERON, Alexander John
„ CAMERON, Edward
Sgt. CAMERON, James
„ CAMERON, Peter Daniel
Pte. CAMILLERI, Benedetto
„ CAMPBELL, Colin Knox
Cpl. CAMPBELL, Colin Stewart
Pte. CAMPBELL, John
L.Cpl. CAMPBELL, John Duncan
Pte. CAMPBELL, John Wilson
„ CAMPBELL, Neil Alexander
Sgt. CAMPBELL, Robert Aubrey F., D.C.M.
Pte. CAMPBELL, William Donald
„ CAMPTON, Cyril
„ CANN, David John
„ CANNON, Reuben Leslie
„ CAREY, Ernest James
Cpl. CARLSON, August Herman
Pte. CARLSON, Martin
„ CARNALL, Charles Thomas
L./Cpl. CARR-BOYD, William Henry
Cpl. CARRIGG, Austin Joseph
„ CARRINGTON, George
Pte. CARROLL, William
„ CARTER, Allan Leslie
„ CARTER, Ernest Henry
„ CARTER, John Lowson
„ CARTER, Roy Foster
„ CASE, Horace Joseph
„ CASEY, Matthew Lionel
„ CASSIDY, William James
„ CAULEY, Thomas
„ CAULFIELD, Thomas Joseph
„ CAVANOUGH, George
„ CAVELL, Walter John
„ CAVEN, Charles
„ CAVENDISH, Harry
Driver CESS, Lewis
Pte. CHADWICK, William John, M.M.
Sgt. CHAILLE, Ernest
Pte. CHALMERS, William
„ CHANDLER, George James
L./Cpl. CHANDLER, Hector
Cpl. CHANDLER, Henry Gregory
Pte. CHAPLAIN, Archibald, Scotland

Pte. CHAPLIN, Charles Edward
„ CHITTICK, Hugh
L./Cpl. CHRISTENSON, Thomas
Pte. CHRISTIE, Edward Mafeking
„ CHRISTIE, Thomas David
„ CLACHER, Leslie James
„ CLANCY, James Joseph
„ CLARK, Cyril Thomas
„ CLARK, John
„ CLARK, John George A.
L./Cpl. CLARK, John
Pte. CLARKE, John
„ CLARKE, Matthew
„ CLARRY, Francis David
„ CLEMO, James Radford
„ CLIFFE, Henry George
„ CLIFFORD, Henry George
„ CLIFFORD, John
„ CLOHERTY, Alexander
„ CLOHESSY, Matthew James
Sgt. CLYDESDALE, David Kennedy
„ COCKSHUTT, William, M.M.
„ COFFEY, John Joseph
„ COFFEY, Patrick
„ COFFEY, Richard Ernest
„ COGDELL, William George
„ COLEBATCH, Harold Gordon
Pte. COLES, Lewis Vincent
„ COLLINS, Alexander Morgan
„ COLLINS, Frank
Cpl. COLLINS, Norman Alfred
Pte. COLLINS, Robert
„ COLLINS, Sydney
„ COLLISON, Arthur Ernest
„ COLMAN, Jack Henry
Sgt. CONDIE, James
Pte. CONDON, Michael John
L./Cpl. CONNOR, John George
Pte. CONROY, Lenny Francis
„ CONSIDINE, Gavin Reginald
„ CONWAY, Joseph Henry
Driver COOK, Hector
Cpl. COOK, Robert, M.M.
Pte. COOMBE, Thomas Joseph
„ COOPER, Cecil Herbert
„ COOPER, Jonathan Leonard
„ COOPER, Joseph William
„ COOPER, Percival
„ COPE, George Edward
L./Cpl. COPELAND, Ralph
Pte. COPELAND, Reginald Heber
„ CORBETT, Alexander
Cpl. CORBETT, Stanley, M.M.
Pte. CORBETT, Thomas Leslie
„ CORDES, Louis Alfred

Pte. CORNEY, John
Sgt. CORNWALL, James Arthur
Cpl. CORRY, William Joseph, M.M.
Pte. COSTELLO, Michael
„ COSTELLO, Martin
„ COSTELLO, Michael Jacob
„ COTTER, Edward
„ COTTERILL, William George
„ COTTRELL, Henry Thomas
„ COUGHLAN, Edward
„ COUGHLIN, Cecil Francis
„ COULTER, George William
Sgt. COURT, William James
Cpl. COUSNER, Arthur Alfred
Pte. COWAN, Lloyd Victor
L.Cpl. CRAWFORD, Robert
Pte. CRAWFORD, Roy
„ CREAN, George
„ CREE, William James
Sgt. CRELLIN, Eric Armistead
Pte. CRETNEY, Thomas Henry
„ CRIBB, Oliver James
„ CRIPPS, William Norman
„ CROOK, Horace Raymond T.
„ CROSS, Alfred Lionel
„ CROSS, William Ernest
Cpl. CROSS, Thomas
Sgt. CROWE, Robert Johnstone, M.M.
Pte. CULLEN, Sydney Raymond
„ CUMES, Harry
„ CUMMINGS, Frederick Joseph
„ CUNNINGHAM, Eugene Martin
„ CURLEY, John Joseph
„ CURRAN, Lionel Slade
„ CURRAN, Patrick
„ CURTIS, George
„ CURTIS, Alexander
„ CUTHBERT, Francis Robert
„ CUTLER, Leslie Thornton
„ DAGG, Roy Edward
L.Cpl. DAHL, William Maurice
Pte. DALEY, Harry Frances
„ DAGLISH, Cecil Dundas
„ DALLIS, Alexander Charles
„ DALY, Hugh Richard
„ DALY, Louis Joseph
Pte. DANCE, Francis Herbert
Sgt. DANIEL, Norman Wesley, M.M.
Pte. DARBY, William Edward
Cpl. DAVEY, Edwin Stanley
Pte. DAVIDSON, Charles William
„ DAVIDSON, William Shiels
„ DAVIDSON, Lovatt
„ DAVIES, Charles
„ DAVIES, Henry

N.C.O.'s AND OTHER RANKS DISCHARGED

L./Cpl. DAVIES, Herbert Montague
„ DAVILL, Robert William E.
Pte. DAVIS, Alexander Thomas
„ DAVIS, Charles
„ DAVIS, Leslie Alexander
Driver DAWES, Frederick William
Pte. DAWSON, James Campbell
„ DAWSON, John Forsyth
Sgt. DAWSON, Robert James
L./Cpl. DAY, Edward Alexander
Sgt. DAY, Phillip Spencer, M.M.
L./Cpl. DAY, Robert William
Cpl. DEEM, William Stanley
L./Cpl. DENNEY, George Montrose
Pte. DENNING, Frederick
„ DENNY, James
„ DEVONSHIRE, Harry
„ DEVONSHIRE, Thomas
„ DEWAR, Alexander
„ DEWING, Arthur
„ DICK, Roy Walter
„ DICK, George Cairney
„ DICKER, George
„ DICKER, Gilbert Hamilton
„ DIMBLEBY, George William
„ DISS, Ronald
„ DIVE, William Evans
„ DIXON, John Henry
„ DOHERTY, Charles Patrick
„ DONAHOO, James Albert
„ DONALDSON, John
Sgt. DONKIN, Cyril, M.M.
Pte. DORMAN, Robert Samuel
„ DORMAN, Reuben Victor
„ DOUGLAS, Harry
„ DOWELL, Peter Reid
„ DOWLING, Henry James
„ DOWNES, John Stuart
„ DOWNES, John William
„ DOWNES, Stanley Hubert
„ DOWNEY, John
„ DOWNS, Charles John
Sgt. DOYLE, Alfred Andrew
Pte. DOYLE, Clarence
Cpl. DOYLE, Charles James
L./Cpl. DOYLE, Eric Leo
Pte. DOYLE, John
„ DOYLE, John Joseph
Cpl. DOYLE, Rexford James E.
L./Cpl. DRABSCH, Arthur Albert
Pte. DRAKE, James
Cpl. DRAPER, Alfred Charles
Pte. DRAPER, Lewis Thomas
„ DRESCHLER, Charles Wagner
Sgt. DREW, Samuel John, M.M.

Sgt. DRYSDALE, John Wirth
Pte. DUFF, D'Arcy Irvine
„ DUFFELL, Phillip Franklin
L./Cpl. DUNCAN, Albert
Pte. DUNCAN, Alexander Maurice
L./Cpl. DUNCAN, James Augustus McD.
Pte. DUNCAN, John Montgomery
„ DUNCAN, Robert
„ DUNCAN, Robert Eli
Sgt. DUNCAN, Walter
Pte. DUNN, Edward George
„ DUNNINGS, Alfred Charles
Sgt. DWYER, Edmund Joseph
Pte. DWYER, Francis Lawrence
„ DWYER, Timothy Joseph, M.M.
L./Cpl. DYER, Walter James
Pte. EALES, Harry John
„ EARLE, Edwin Percival
„ EARL, William Henry
„ EASTEN, William Edward
„ EDDINGTON, Charles Edward
L./Cpl. EDMISTONE, Alexander Murdoch
Pte. EDWARDS, Austin Lismore
„ EDWARDS, Edward
Sgt. EDWARDS, James Elton
Pte. EDWARDS, Thomas Harold
„ EGAN, William Andrew
„ EGGINS, Eric Stanley
„ EGGINS, Ira Cressy
„ EGGLETON, Albert George
„ EISING, William Frederick, M.M.
„ ELLAM, Arthur Harold
„ ELLIOTT, Archibald John
„ ELLIOTT, Sidney
„ ELLIOTT, Arthur Thomas
„ ELLIOTT, William
„ ELLIS, Francis Lambert
„ ELLIS, George Douglas,
„ ELLIS, John Henry
„ ELMES, Albert Alfred
„ ERNST, Frederick Otto
„ EVANS, Thomas Joseph
Cpl. EVANS, William Edward
Pte. EXTON, William Thomas
„ EVEREST, Walter
„ FAGAN, John Valentine
„ FAGG, Charles Graham
Sgt. FAHEY, William, M.M. and Bar
„ FAHEY, William Joseph
Pte. FAIRFULL, John
L./Cpl. FALLOWS, Herbert
Pte. FALVEY, Edward
„ FANCOURT, Robert Gregson

Pte. FARLEY, Frederick William
„ FARMER, Ernest
„ FARNELL, Arthur
„ FARQUHAR, James Jarrow
Sgt. FARRELL, David
Pte. FARRELL, James
Q.M.S. FEARNSIDE, Henry
Pte. FEATHERSTONE, Percy George
„ FEDRICK, William Henry
„ FALLOWS, William Alexander
Cpl. FERGUSON, Archie George V.
Pte. FERGUSON, Charles Dennis
„ FERGUSON, Richard Albert, M.M.
„ FERNIE, James
„ FERRICKS, Michael John
„ FINLAYSON, Frank Japp
„ FISCHER, Maurice Bertram
„ FISHER, Leslie George
L./Cpl. FITT, Robert David
Pte. FITZGERALD, George James
„ FITZGERALD, James Joseph
Cpl. FITZGERALD, Thomas Lattin
Cpl. FITZPATRICK, Luke
Pte. FIXTER, Charles Langley
Cpl. FLEGG, Sydney Frank
Pte. FLEMMING, Alexander
„ FLETCHER, James Frederick
„ FLYNN, William Henry
„ FOLKES, Cecil James
„ FOLKES, Francis Lloyd
„ FORBES, Archibald Albert
„ FORBES, Charles Bowers
Cpl. FORD, Henry Hugh
Pte. FORD, John
„ FORD, Victor
„ FORD, William
„ FORD, William George
„ FORMAN, William
„ FORSHAW, William Henry
L./Cpl. FORSTER, Richard
Pte. FOSTER, Kenneth John Henry
„ FOSTER, Walter
Sgt. FOWLER, Spencer William
Pte. FOWLER, William James
„ FOX, Anthony John
„ FOX, Edwin Gladwin
„ FRAMPTON, Francis Roy
„ FRANCIS, John
„ FRANKLIN, John Frederick
„ FRASER, Arthur William
„ FRASER, Harry
„ FRASER, Thomas Angus
„ FRASER, William
„ FREDERICK, Homer Campbell

Pte. FREDERICKS, Francis Clarence
„ FREEMAN, Arthur Frederick
„ FROST, John Frederick
„ FURMAN, Henry Garfield
Driver FURNISS, Edgar
Pte. FURNIVALL, Percival
Sgt. FYLES, Ernest Alfred
Pte. FYSH, Arthur Kershaw
„ GALLAGHER, Arthur Haslam
„ GALLOWAY, John
„ GALLOWAY, Peter
„ GARDENER, Henry Charles
„ GARDNER, Harold
„ GARDNER, Robert
Sgt. GARDNER, William Elliott
Pte. GARNER, Alfred
„ GARNER, Frederick William
L./Cpl. GARRETT, Herbert Henry
Pte. GARVIS, Edwin Thomas
„ GATES, Alfred Mulgrave D.
Q.M.S. GEISE, Frederick
Pte. GEIZER, Thomas William
„ GEMMELL, John Curry
„ GEORGANTIS, George
L./Cpl. GERRARD, John Frederick
Pte. GIBBS, Ernest George
„ GIBSON, Alfred
„ GIELIS, Arthur Ernest
„ GIESEMANN, George
„ GILBRIDE, Bernard Joseph
„ GILES, John
„ GILL, Albert
„ GILL, Benjamin
„ GILL, Walter
„ GILLESPIE, Henry William G.
„ GILLESPIE, Joseph
„ GILLESPIE, Richard, M.M.
„ GILMORE, Sydney Wilton
„ GLASBY, Frederick
„ GLASBY, Robert William
„ GLEDHILL, Henry
„ GLEESON, Charles
„ GLEESON, William
L./Cpl. GOOD, Samuel Alfred R.
Pte. GOODALL, Albert Edward
Driver GOODGER, Walter George
L./Cpl. GOODLAND, William Albert, M.M.
Pte. GOODWIN, Charles Herbert
„ GOODWIN, Edward
Pte. GORMLEY, Patrick Joseph
Sgt. GOSS, Francis James
Pte. GOUGH, Arthur Walter
„ GOULD, Leslie Walter
„ GRACE, Edward

N.C.O.'s AND OTHER RANKS DISCHARGED

Pte. GRAHAM, Albert Thomas
Sgt. GRAHAM, Edgar Richard, M.M.
Pte. GRAHAM, Harold
Cpl. GRAHAM, Rowland Montrose
L./Cpl. GRAHAM, Sydney George
Pte. GRAINGER, William
Cpl. GRAMBOWER, George Robert
Pte. GRANT, James
L./Cpl. GRANT, Malcolm Fraser
Pte. GRANT, Robert Gustavus
,, GRAY, Harold Hereward
Q.M.S. GRAY, Robert Chalmers
Pte. GRAY, Thomas
Cpl. GRAY, Walter
Driver GRAY, Walter Cecil
Pte. GREAVES, Owen Vernon
,, GREBERT, Henry Michael
,, GREEN, Charles Henry
,, GREEN, Albert Edward
,, GREENHALPH, Joseph
Sgt. GREER, Henry, D.C.M.
Pte. GREIG, Arthur Roy A.
Cpl. GREINER, Leonard Carr
Pte. GRENDON, William Lewis, M.M.
,, GRIFFIN, Cecil George
,, GRIFFITH, Gilmour
,, GRIFFITHS, Charles
,, GRIFFITHS, Christopher James
,, GRIFFITHS, George
,, GRIFFITHS, James Patrick
,, GRIFFITHS, Laurence Edward
,, GROOM, John George
,, GROSSE, William Edward
Sgt. GROTH, Roland
Pte. GROTH, William Leo
,, GROUNDWATER, James Cargill
,, GROUNDWATER, James Robert
,, GRUNDY, Harold
,, GUBBINS, William
,, GUEST, Godfrey Henry
L./Cpl. GUNDRY, Cecil Charles
Pte. GUY, William Hutchinson
,, GUYATT, Albert Edgar
,, GWYNNE, Harold Thomas
,, HACKETT, John Canham
,, HADEN, Charles William
,, HAIGH, James Wilfred
,, HAINES, Herbert Cecil
Cpl. HAIR, Andrew Love
Pte. HAIR, John Milroy
L./Cpl. HAIR, Robert
Pte. HALES, Frederick Thomas
,, HALL, Charles
,, HALL, Clarence James
,, HALL, Duncan

Pte. HALL, Herbert James
Cpl. HALL, Robert Galt
Pte. HALL, Ulric Roy
,, HALL, Warry
,, HALLIDAY, Frederick William
Cpl. HAMMOND, William Henry
Pte. HAMPSON, Thomas John P.
,, HANCOCK, David Theophilus
,, HANDLEY, Frederick Charles
,, HANLON, George Macqueen S.
,, HANNIGAN, Maurice Cecil
,, HANSEN, Arthur D.
Pte. HANSEN, Charles
,, HANSEN, Neils William
,, HANSEN, Robert Bernart
,, HANSEN, Simon Julius
,, HANSEN, William
Cpl. HANSEN, Henrick Pear
,, HANSON, Leonard Peter
L./Cpl. HARDIE, Thomas Gibson
Pte. HARDY, Sidney Albert
,, HARE, John, M.M.
Sgt. HARMAN, Edgar Ernest,
M.M. and Bar.
Pte. HARMSTON, John Stanley
,, HARMSWORTH, Samuel Charles
Driver HARPER, Alfred George
Pte. HARPER, Charles
,, HARRINGTON, Charles
Sgt. HARRIS, Charles Frederick, M.M.
Pte. HARRIS, Francis Small
,, HARRIS, George Arthur
,, HARRIS, John Reece
,, HARRIS, Norman Rackley
,, HART, Stuart Esmonde T.
,, HARTWIG, Charles
,, HARVEY, Arthur
,, HARVEY, Christian William
,, HARVEY, James
Cpl. HASKINS, William, M.M.
Pte. HAWKINS, Albert
,, HAWKINS, Reginald Francis
,, HAY, John
,, HAY, James
,, HAY, Leslie Albert
,, HAYES, Walter James
,, HAYES, Arthur Edward
,, HAYWOOD, Benjamin
,, HEAD, Ernest
,, HEALY, John Kelly
L./Cpl. HELTON, Eustace Cyril N.
Pte. HENDERSON, John
,, HENDERSON, Thomas Archibald
,, HENDRY, Leo James
L./Cpl. HENDRY, William

Pte. HENRICKS, David Nicholas
„ HEPPER, William Henry
„ HEPWORTH, Wilfred Edward
„ HERBERT, Joseph
„ HERON, Elsdon
Cpl. HESLOP, Albert Donald
Pte. HESSEY, Bernard
„ HICK, Thomas
„ HICKEY, Cornelius Joseph
„ HICKS, Austin William
„ HIFTON, Herbert
Driver HIGGINS, Thomas Herbert
L./Cpl. HILL, Bryson
Pte. HILL, George Arthur
Cpl. HILL, Joseph Warren
Driver HILL, Percy
Pte. HILL, William Henry C.
„ HILLCOAT, Claude Robert
„ HILLMAN, Samuel Benjamin
„ HILLS, Frederick Edward
„ HILLS, George Thomas
„ HINCHLIFF, Percy
„ HINDS, James
„ HINKLER, Jack William
„ HINTZ, Frederick
„ HOARE, Charles Frederick
„ HOBSON, William
L./Cpl. HOCKINGS, Franklin Herbert
Sgt. HODGETTS, Arthur Thomas
Cpl. HOFF, August Johan
Pte. HODSON, Walter Cyril
Col. HOLLAND, Cyril Thomas
Pte. HOLLAND, Gwilym Ernest
L./Cpl. HOLLOWAY, Thomas Leonard, D.C.M.
Pte. HOLT, Leslie
L./Cpl. HOME, Leslie Cameron
Pte. HONEY, Charles Staving
„ HONEYWILL, William
„ HOOK, James
„ HOPE, John Robert
„ HOPGOOD, Thomas John
„ HOPKINS, Albert Carlyle
„ HOPKINS, Jack Escott
L./Cpl. HOPKINS, Stanley John
Pte. HORNE, William George
Pte. HOUGHTON, Bertie Gregory
Driver HOULAHAN, Jack
„ HOURIGAN, Robert Edward
Pte. HOUSTON, James
„ HOUSTON, William
„ HOWARD, Thomas McLennan W.
Sgt. HOWE, Herbert George
Pte. HOWIE, Alexander
„ HOWLAND, Sydney James

Pte. HUBBARD, Albert
„ HUDSON, John
„ HUDSON, John Harold
„ HUET, Harry Victor
Cpl. HUGHES, Frederick Charles
Pte. HUGHES, John Edward
„ HUGHES, Thomas
Driver HUGHES, William John
„ HULCOMBE, William Milford
Pte. HUMBER, Ernest Negus
„ HUMPHREYS, Edward Leichardt
Cpl. HUNGERFORD, Sydney Gordon
Pte. HUNT, Richard Harold
„ HUNTER, Alexander
„ HURLEY, James
„ HURLEY, Patrick
„ HURST, Richard William
„ HURST, Thomas Hilton
„ HUSSON, George
„ HUTCHINS, Leo Francis
Cpl. HUTCHINSON, James, M.M.
Pte. HYNES, James
„ IDLE, Frederick Arthur
R.Q.M.S. INGLIS, Reginald Alfred
Pte. IRELAND, Albert Edward
„ IRONMONGER, Robert George
„ IRONMONGER, Thomas
„ IRVING, Robert
„ IVEY, Phillip
„ IVORY, Campbell Holmes
L./Cpl. JACKLIN, Abe
Sgt. JACKSON, George Albert
Pte. JAKEMAN, Andrew, M.S.M.
„ JAKEMAN, Percy
Sgt. JAMES, Alexander William
Pte. JAMES, John William
„ JACQUES, Wilfred Charles
„ JACQUES, Wilfred Leslie
„ JARRETT, James Thomas
„ JARVIS, Victor Henry
„ JARVIS, Jesse Charles
Cpl. JARVIS, Patrick
Pte. JEFFREY, Robert
„ JENNINGS, Frederick Frank
„ JENNINGS, Ventry Clarence
„ JENSEN, Hans Peter
„ JEROME, Norman Joseph
„ JINKINS, Roy
„ JOHNS, William James
„ JOHNSON, Joseph
„ JOHNSON, Norman Harold
„ JOHNSON, Stephen
„ JOHNSON, William
„ JOHNSTON, George Boyd
„ JOHNSTON, Joseph

N.C.O.'s AND OTHER RANKS DISCHARGED

Sgt. JOHNSTON, Leslie Harold
Pte. JOHNSTON, Samuel Joseph
Cpl. JOHNSTONE, Herbert Mitchell
Pte. JOHNSTONE, James
   „ JOHNSTONE, John Thomas
L./Cpl. JOLLY, Gervaise Esdaile, C. de G.
Pte. JOICE, Alfred George
   „ JONES, Clarence
   „ JONES, David Francis
   „ JONES, Frederick
   „ JONES, John Reid
Sgt. JONES, Percy Sutherland
Pte. JONES, Paul Wesley
   „ JONES, Rueben Trappett
   „ JONES, Samuel James
   „ JONES, Thomas
   „ JONES, William Charles
   „ JONES, Wilfred John
Driver JORGENSEN, James Axel A.
Pte. JORGENSEN, John Hans
Q.M.S. JORGENSEN, James Peter
Cpl. JOWETT, Victor Dawson
Cpl. JOYCE, David Joseph
Pte. JOYCE, Robert
   „ JUDD, Albert
W.O. (1) JUDD, William James, M.M.
Pte. JUNNER, James Andrew
   „ KADEL, Gilbert Stanley
L./Cpl. KEANE, Michael
Pte. KEARIN, John
   „ KEARNEY, Denis George
Sgt. KEARNEY, Joseph, M.I.D.
Pte. KEARNEY, William Arthur
   „ KEATING, Ronald Vivian
   „ KEEP, Wesley Simmonds
Driver KEIGHTLEY, Charles
Pte. KELLY, Edward Albert
Sgt. KELLY, Edwin Lang, M.S.M.
Pte. KELLY, Joepeh Mervyn
   „ KELLY, James Thomas
L./Cpl. KELLY, John William J.
Pte. KELLY, Laurence
Driver KELLY, Martin
Pte. KELLY, William
Sgt. KELLY, William Charles
Pte. KELLY, William John
   „ KELLY, William Thomas
   „ KELSO, Alexander
   „ KEMP, Edwin
   „ KEMP, James
   „ KENNEALLY, John Alexander
   „ KENNEDY, William James
   „ KENNEDY, William Roy
   „ KENT, John Hugh R.

Pte. KENYON, James Stanley
   „ KERNAHAN, James Joseph
   „ KERTON, John
   „ KEYS, Francis William
   „ KIDD, Ernest Phillip
   „ KIDD, Thomas Coleman
L./Cpl. KILMARTIN, Leslie Joseph
Pte. KILPIN, Cyril Douglas
   „ KIM, William John, M.M.
Driver KING, Ernest King
Pte. KING, George
   „ KING, George Frederick
   „ KING, Harold
Sgt. KING, Hunter Stanley
Pte. KING, William
   „ KINGSTON, Francis Charles
   „ KINGSTON, Frederick George
   „ KINGSTON, John Henry
   „ KIRBY, Walter
   „ KIRKPATRICK, Alexander
   „ KIRKPATRICK, James Alexander
L./Cpl. KIRWIN, Dick
Pte. KITE, Walter Thomas
   „ KLAUKE, Gustav
Sgt. KLEMM, Stanley Karl
Pte. KLEVE, William Heinrich, M.M.
   „ KLING, Victor Edward N.
   „ KNIGHT, Charles
   „ KNIGHT, John William
   „ KOPPE, Frederick
   „ KUNKLER, Frederick Charles
   „ LACEY, Thomas Kingsmill
   „ LAING, Thomas Knight
   „ LAKE-HARCOURT, Edgar Sydney
   „ LAMB, James
   „ LAMB, Herbert William A.
   „ LAMBERT, Albert Edward
   „ LAMBERT, Berkeley Arthur
Driver LAMBERT, Henry
Pte. LANG, Leslie George
   „ LANG, William
   „ LANGDON, James Conway
   „ LARDER, Thomas William
Q.M.S. LARKIN, William Arthur
Pte. LATHANGIE, David
Cpl. LATTIN, John Antonius
Pte. LAURENCESON, Rueben
   „ LAWSON, Peter
   „ LAWTON, Edward James
W.O. (2) LAYFIELD, Frederick Charles
Pte. LE BHERS, Alfred Henry
   „ LEE, Archibald Thompson
   „ LEE, James Alexander

Pte. LEE, William Frederick
Cpl. LEIGHTON, John, M.M.
Pte. LEITCH, Angus
L./Cpl. LENMAN, William Leonard
„ LEONARD, Leonard
Pte. LESTER, Albert Gladstone
Cpl. LEWIS, Ernest Leonard
Pte. LEWIS, Henry Colin
„ LIGHT, Charles
„ LINDSAY, Erle Thomas
„ LINDSAY, Raymond John
Cpl. LITTLETON, Roland Edward
Pte. LITZOW, Robert August
„ LIVINGSTONE, Malcolm
„ LIVINGSTONE, Stanley
„ LOBB, Henry
L./Cpl. LOBLEY, John Arthur
Pte. LOCHRAN, Robert John
„ LOFTHOUSE, Joseph
„ LONG, Frederick Thomas
„ LONG, Henry Howard
„ LONG, Roy Harold
Sgt. LOUGHEED, Henry Jesse F.
Pte. LOVE, Frank
„ LOVERING, William Francis
Sgt. LOWE, John Edward
Pte. LUCAS, William Alfred
Sgt. LUSCOMBE, Leslie George
Pte. LUXON, Arthur Ernest
„ LYNCH, Frank
„ LYNCH, Harold James
„ LYNCH, John Joseph
Cpl. MACCOLL, Archibald Robertson
Pte. MACCOLL, John
„ MACDONALD, Colin Campbell
„ MACDONALD, Donald
„ MACIVER, Murdock
Sgt. MACKENZIE, George Rose
Pte. MACINTOSH, Angus
L./Cpl. MACPHERSON, Alexander
Pte. MADDEN, Harold Rupert
„ MAGARRY, Ernest George
„ MAHER, Clarence Garnet
Sgt. MAHONEY, Robert
Q.M.S. MAIN, Harry Edward
Pte. MAKAROF, George
„ MALCOLM, William
„ MALONE, Frank
„ MALONE, Peter
L./Cpl. MANN, John Henry, D.C.M., M.M.
Pte. MANSON, Thomas Henry
„ MARKS, Herbert Henry
„ MARKWELL, William Sherman
Sgt. MARRIAN, Frank William, M.M.

Pte. MARSDEN, Alexander
„ MARSH, Arthur Frederick
„ MARSH, Benjamin, M.M.
„ MARSH, Louis John
„ MARSH, Walter
„ MARSHALL, Robert
„ MARTIN, Frank Sydney
„ MARTIN, John Bertram
Driver MARTIN, Noble Elliott
Pte. MARTYR, James
„ MATCHEN, Arthur
„ MATHESON, Robert Foxgrave
Driver MATTHEWSON, Robert
Pte. MATTHEWS, Edward Ashby
„ MATTHEWS, Colin Abraham
„ MATTHEWS, Thomas
Cpl. MAUNDER, Jack Purdy
Pte. MAWHINNEY, Thomas
L./Cpl. MAXWELL, Albert Wyndham
Pte. MAXWELL, Robert Clarke
Sgt. MAYES, William Edmond
Pte. MAYNARD, Sydney Thomas
L./Cpl. MEARS, Douglas
Pte. MEARS, Edmond Patrick
L./Cpl. MEARS, George
Pte. MEARS, Mark
„ MEDDLETON, Robert Hartley
„ MEEHAN, John Francis
„ MEIER, Carl
Sgt. MELLOY, Robert Sydney
L./Cpl. MELSOM, Frank
Pte. MENGEL, Charles Frederick
„ MERCER, Charles Ezekial
„ MEREDITH, Alfred
„ MESKELL, Ernest Edward
„ METCALFE, Joseph
„ MEW, William Stanley
„ MICHAEL, Edgar William
„ MIDDLETON, George Edward
„ MIDGLEY, William Barron, M.M.
Sgt. MILES, Walter John
Pte. MILLER, Frank
„ MILLER, Charles Spiers
„ MILLER, Henry Moring
„ MILLER, James
„ MILLER, Michael Joseph
Sgt. MILLER, Peter Stewart
Pte. MILLER, Robert George
„ MILLER, Robert John
„ MILLER, Valentine Nevil
„ MILLENGEN, Arthur Claude
L./Cpl. MILLWARD, Reginald Ronald
Pte. MILNE, Edward Alexander
„ MILNE, William
Cpl. MINCHIN, Noel Beechey

N.C.O.'s AND OTHER RANKS DISCHARGED 149

L./Cpl. MINERS, Victor Sydney
Pte. MITCHELL, Evan William
     " MITCHELL, Norman Spencer
Driver MITCHELL, Robert James
Pte. MITCHELL, Sydney
     " MITCHELL, William Robert
     " MOIR, James
     " MONAGHAN, Robert
     " MOORCROFT, Robert Archibald
     " MOORE, George Roland, M.M.
     " MOORE, Robert Joseph
     " MORE, William Percy
     " MOREFIELD, John
     " MORGAN, George
Sgt. MORGAN, George Evan, M.M. and Bar.
Pte. MORGAN, John Edgar
     " MORGAN, William Ambrose
     " MORLEY, Alexander
     " MORRIS, Alexander John
     " MORRIS, Cornelius Ambrose
     " MORRIS, Richard George
     " MORRIS, Harry
     " MORRIS, Thomas John
     " MORRIS, William James
     " MORRISON, Edwin Alexander
L./Cpl. MORRISON, Sydney Erskine, M.M.
Pte. MORSE, Oswald Hector
     " MOSS, Ernest John
     " MOSS, Herbert William R.
     " MOULDS, Joseph Welby
     " MUIR, Herbert Angus
Cpl. MULLAN, Bernard John
Pte. MULLAN, Michael
     " MULRENAN, Arthur Reginald
     " MUNDT, Louis Fritz
     " MUNRO, David
Sgt. MUNRO, Donald Allan
Pte. MUNRO, Hugo
     " MUNRO, John James
Sgt. MUNRO, Victor Lee
Pte. MUNRO, William James
     " MURISON, William Stewart
Driver MURPHY, James
Pte. MURPHY, James
     " MURPHY, Morris Vincent
     " MURRAY, Allan
     " MURRAY, Bernard
     " MURRAY, Frank Veitch
     " MURRAY, John
L./Cpl. MURRAY, Norman Stanley, M.M.
Pte. MURTAGH, Michael Joseph D.
     " MURTON, Arthur Samual

Pte. MURTON, Victor Harold
     " McALEESE, William John
     " McCABE, John
L./Cpl. McCASKER, James Gildas
Pte. McCASKER, Richard Henry
     " McCLAY, Joseph Patrick
     " McCLYMONT, Edward Victor
     " McCOLL, Allan
     " McCOMBE, Robert
     " McCONNELL, Arthur Eric
     " McCONNELL, John Joseph
     " McCORMICK, Thomas Austin
     " McCREATH, Charles
     " McCULLOCH, John
L./Cpl. McCUSKER, Anthony Joseph
Pte. McDONALD, Alexander
     " McDONALD, John
     " McDONALD, Robert Leslie G.
L./Cpl. McDONALD, Roy Sinclair
Pte. McDONALD, William
     " McDONALD, William Arthur
     " McDONNELL, Daniel
     " McDONNELL, Kieran
L.Cpl. McDONOUGH, Francis Patrick
Pte. McDONOUGH, Charles Thomas
     " McDONOUGH, Martin
Cpl. McERLANE, William James
Pte. McEVOY, Patrick Thomas
     " McFADDEN, Clealand George
     " McGAVIN, Robert Ernest
     " McGAW, Thomas
Sgt. McGHIE, Edwin
Pte. McGINITY, Patrick
     " McGUINESS, Leslie
     " McGUINESS, Stanley
     " McGLAVE, Peter Leo
     " McGREGOR, Donald Roy, M.M.
     " McGUINESS, Bernard
L./Cpl. McGUIRE, Leonard George
Pte. McGUIRE, Thomas, M.I.D.
     " McINNES, William
     " McINTOSH, Alexander
     " McINTOSH, James Shaw
     " McIVOR, Edward John
     " McKAY, Donald
Cpl. McKEAN, William James B.
Pte. McKEE, Patrick
     " McKELVIE, William
     " McKENZIE, Alexander Forrest
     " McKENZIE, Daniel
     " McKENZIE, John Findlay
     " McKENZIE, Kenneth
     " McKERR, Matthew
     " McKIE, Arthur

Pte. McKINNON, Percy
„ McKINNON, Victor Tasman
„ McLACHLAN, Arthur Hector
„ McLAREN, James William
Driver McLAREN, Donald, M.M.
Cpl. McLAREN, Peter Donald
Pte. McLEAN, Joseph Benton
„ McLEAN, John Crichton
„ McLEAN, Roger Warwick
„ McLEAN, William Douglas
„ McLELLAN, Robert Hall
„ McLENNAN, John Kenneth
Cpl. McLIVER, Kenneth Gordon
„ McLOUGHLIN, Thomas Daniel
Pte. McMACHON, Francis
„ McMACKIN, Patrick
„ McMANUS, James George
„ McMANUS, Thomas
L./Cpl. McMANUS, William David
Pte. McMILLAN, Reginald Percy
„ McMILLAN, Cecil Herbert
Cpl. McNAUGHT, Arthur Stanley
Pte. McNIELL, Richard
„ McNEVEN, Charles Alexander
L./Cpl. McPHEE, Donald Beatson
Pte. McPHERSON, Archie
„ McPHERSON, Francis
Cpl. McPHERSON, Hector
Pte. McCREADY, Thomas Ambrose
„ McROBBIE, John
„ McRORY, John Joseph
„ McVEIGH, George
„ McWATTERS, Peter Hannah
„ McWATTERS, Agesilaus, M.M.
„ NALDER, Alfred
„ NARBOROUGH, Roy St. Clair
„ NATION, Charles Norman
„ NAYLOR, Herbert Alfred, M.M.
„ NEALE, Cecil
„ NEALE, Sydney George
„ NEIGHBOUR, Sydney Claude
„ NEVIN, George Henry
Cpl. NEW, Arthur George
L./Cpl. NEWBERY, Leslie Arthur
Pte. NEWBERY, Stanley Buchanan
„ NEWELL, Augustus McKean
„ NEWMAN, Charles
„ NEWMAN, Patrick
„ NEWTON, Augustus John
„ NICHOLSON, George William
Sgt. NICOL, George Hunter L.
Pte. NILSON, Neil Henry
„ NIPPERESS, Thomas Alfred
Cpl. NOBLE, Robert
Pte. NOLAN, Arthur

Pte. NOLAN, Charles
„ NOLAN, Edward
„ NOLAN, Francis Stephen
„ NONMUS, Gilbert Brierly
„ NORTH, Edward Donald
„ NOYES, George
„ OAKDEN, John Robert
„ OAKHILL, William Perkins
„ O'BRIEN, Charles Edward
Sgt. O'BRIEN, Francis
Pte. O'BRIEN, John Robert
„ O'BRIEN, Robert Michael
L./Cpl. O'BRIEN, Thomas Walter
„ O'BRIEN, William, M.M.
Pte. O'BRYAN, Andrew James
„ O'CALLAGHAN, John
„ O'CONNELL, James
„ O'DONNELL, Daniel Joseph
Driver O'DRISCOLL, John
Pte. O'DRISCOLL, Thomas
Driver OGG, Gordon Alexander
Pte. OGG, James William
Cpl. O'GORMAN, Peter
L./Cpl. O'GRADY, William John
Pte. O'KEEFE, Daniel
„ O'KEEFE, Patrick Michael
„ OLDHAM, George
„ OLIVE, Malcolm Alexander
„ OLIVER, John Harold
„ OLLEY, Joseph Daniel
„ OLSEN, Fredrik Adolf
„ OLSEN, Niels
„ OLSEN, Severin
„ O'MEARA, Michael Francis
Sgt. O'NEILL, John Alphonsus
Pte. O'NEILL, Lionel
„ ORD, Percy Marstin
„ O'REILLY, John
„ O'REILLY, Joseph
„ O'REILLY, John
„ ORLOFF, Steven
„ O'ROURKE, John Percival
„ OSBOURNE, Fred Harrison
„ O'SHANNESSY, Stephen James
„ O'SULLIVAN, John
„ O'SULLIVAN, Mortimer
„ O'SULLIVAN, Michael Patrick
„ O'SULLIVAN, Richard
„ O'SULLIVAN, Timothy
„ OUTRIDGE, James Gordon
„ OVENDEN, Thomas William L.
„ OWEN, Edward
Cpl. PACKMAN, Albert Edward
Sgt. PAGE, Clive Basil
Pte. PAGE, John Edmond

N.C.O.'s AND OTHER RANKS DISCHARGED

Pte. PAGE, Samuel
„ PAINE, Maitland Richard S.
Pte. PALMER, Alfred
„ PALMER, Frank
„ PALMER, Joseph Leslie N.
„ PALMER, John Woodford
„ PALMER, Thomas Henry E.
„ PALMER, Vivian Loftus
„ PARKER, John James
„ PARKER, Raymond Horace
„ PARRY, George Edward
„ PARSONS, Bertrid John
„ PARSONS, George Henry
„ PARSONS, Sydney Albert
„ PASCOE, Herbert
„ PASHLEY, William
„ PATTERSON, John Etheridge
Sgt. PATTERSON, Kenneth George, M.M.
Cpl. PATTISON, Herbert John
Pte. PAUL, Michael
L./Cpl. PAYNE, Charles
Pte. PAYNE, Keith Bart
„ PAYNE, Thomas Basil
Sgt. PEACOCK, John Clarence, M.M.
Pte. PEACOCK, James Howard S.
„ PEAKE, James Walter
„ PEARSON, Reginald John
„ PEARSON, William Thomas
Cpl. PEDLER, Walter
Pte. PEDWELL, Walter Henry
L./Cpl. PENDER, Bernard
Sgt. PENDER, John
Pte. PENNEFATHER, Edward Kingsmill
„ PENNICOTT, Reginald Hale
„ PERKINS, Leonard George
Sgt. PERKINS, William Brown
Pte. PERREN, Frederick John
„ PERRY, Ernest
L./Cpl. PETERS, John Thomas, M.M.
Pte. PETERSON, Harry
Sgt. PETERSON, Joseph Emanuel
Pte. PHILLIPS, Henry
„ PHILLIPS, Josslyn
„ PHILLIPS, Joseph William
L./Cpl. PHILLIPS, Percy Wenham
Pte. PHIPPS, George Henry
L./Cpl. PIKE, Lindsay Thomas
Pte. PINKERTON, John Howe
„ PITT, George
„ PLEAVIN, Reginald Donald
„ PODOSKY, Horace Marcus
„ POKARIER, Henry
„ PONTING, Edward

Pte. POOL, John Herbert
„ POPE, Walter James
Cpl. POPHAM, Robert Benjamin
Pte. POWELL, George
Cpl. POWELL, Harry
L./Cpl. POWELL, Victor George
Pte. POWELL, William Leonard
„ POWER, Thomas Michael
„ POWER, William Frederick J.
Cpl. PRATT, Arthur Lacombie
Pte. PRATT, George Edward
„ PREBBLE, Edward
„ PRESTON, Bertram
„ PRICE, Daniel Thomas
„ PRICE, Josiah
L./Cpl. PRICE, James John
Pte. PRICE, Richard
„ PRICE, William
„ PRIOR, Frederick
„ PRIOR, Lawrence
„ PUKALLUS, Albert Edward
L./Cpl. PULLEN, Charles
Pte. PULLEN, Jenkin William
„ PULLEN, Robert
„ PURTLE, Robert
„ PUTT, George William
Sgt. QUIGLEY, Peter
Pte. QUILTER, John Vincent
„ QUINLAN, Norman Anthony
„ QUINN, Thomas Joseph
„ QUINN, William Farncis
„ QUIRK, Patrick Thomas
„ RAFTER, John Joseph
Sgt. RAGH, Albert William
L./Cpl. RAKE, Charles Albert
Pte. RAKE, James Vivian
„ RAMSAY, John
„ RAMSAY, James Alfred
„ RAMSAY, James Penman
„ RAMSDEN, Robert Burns
„ RAMSHAW, Albert
„ RANDALL, Frederick John
„ RANSON, Samuel
L./Cpl. RAPKINS, Herbert Tangney
Pte. RASEY, Thomas William
„ RATCLIFFE, William Thomas
C.S.M. RATTEN, Arthur Guy
Sgt. READ, George James H., D.C.M., M.M.
Pte. READ, Robert
„ READY, John
„ REARDON, Albert John
„ REDDING, Francis
Cpl. REE, Sydney James

W.O. REED, William Thomas, M.M. and Bar.
Pte. REEVES, Thomas Jeremiah
„ REID, Clarence Andrew
„ REID, John
„ REID Maurice
„ REID, Oswald Morris
„ REID, Stewart
„ REID, William
„ REID, Wilson Irwin
„ RENDOTH, Albert
„ REYNOLDS, Anthony
„ REYNOLDS, Herbert Sidney
L./Cpl. REYNOLDS, James Montague
Pte. REYNOLDS, Thomas Jerome
„ RHODES, Frederick William A.
„ RICHARDS, George William C.
„ RICHARDS, Ishmail David J.
„ RICHARDS, Thomas
„ RICHARDSON, Barrington William
„ RICHARDSON, George
„ RICHARDSON, Peter Stanley
„ RICKETTS, James Christopher
„ RIDLEY, Maurice John
„ REILLY, Sydney Francis
„ RIGGALL, John William
„ RITCHIE, Robert Charles F.
„ RITCHIE, William Roy
„ ROACH, Michael
„ ROACH, Michael Joseph
L./Cpl. ROACH, Thomas
Pte. ROBB, Percy
„ ROBERTS, Charles James
„ ROBERTS, Frank
„ ROBERTS, Luke
„ ROBERTS, Walter Sheldon
„ ROBERTSON, Archibald Campbell
Sgt. ROBERTSON, John
„ ROBERTSON, James
„ ROBERTSON, John
Pte. ROBERTSON, James Wood
Cpl. ROBINSON, Alfred
Pte. ROBINSON, Henry Charles
„ ROBINSON, John Joseph
„ ROBINSON, William Henry O.
„ ROBINSON, Wilfred Gerald
„ ROBSON, William Charles
„ ROE, William Freemantle
Cpl. ROBINSON, Cyril
Pte. ROLFE, Augustine Pius
„ ROLFE, William Finnin R.
„ ROOKE, John Allan
„ ROSE, Charles Alfred

Pte. ROSE, Frederick, M.M.
„ ROSE, Lawrence Albert
„ ROSE, Norman Winton
„ ROSS, David George
„ ROSS, Ernest John
„ ROSS, Frederick George
„ ROSS, Gordon
„ ROSSITER, Percy
„ ROUNTREE, Thomas
L./Cpl. ROWE, John Henry
Pte. ROWLAND, Ivor
„ RUDGE, George Thomas
„ RUMP, Arnold William
„ RUSH, Albert
„ RUSSELL, James Reginald
Sgt. RUSSELL, Sydney
Pte. RUTHERFORD, Robert Edwin, M.I.D.
„ RYAN, Matthew
„ RYANS, William
„ RYDER, George
„ SAIT, Charles Walter H.
„ SALKELD, Benjamin Hubert
„ SALTMARSH, Alfred Edward
Sapper SAINTY, Harry
L./Cpl. SALTZER, Ludie Emil
Pte. SAMMON, Patrick Daniel
„ SANDERS, Edward Harold
L./Cpl. SANDERS, Oscar
„ SANDILANDS, Adam Brownlie
Pte. SANKEY, John Herbert
„ SAUNDERS, George Joseph
„ SAUNDERS, John
Pte. SAUNDERS, William Arthur
„ SAVAGE, David
„ SAVAGE, Percival Douglas, M.M.
Sgt. SCANLON, Bernard, M.I.D.
Pte. SCHAFFER, Albert Eric V.
„ SCHMIDT, Niels Kristen
„ SCHOLES, Richard Norton M.
„ SCHWINGHAMMER, Verdi George
„ SCOTT, William
„ SCRAGG, Albert Edward
„ SEABROOK, Percy
„ SEAMAN, Henry Arthur B.
„ SEPPLE, Henry, M.M.
„ SEYMOUR, George Emanuel
„ SEYMOUR, George Henry A.
„ SHAMBROOK, Samuel Ernest
„ SHANNON, William Patrick
„ SHAPCOTT, Harold Sutton
„ SHEARIN, Ambrose Dominic
Cpl. SHELTON, William
Pte. SHEPARD, Edward

N.C.O.'s AND OTHER RANKS DISCHARGED

Pte. SHEPPARD, Joseph Henry G.
" SHEPPARD, John Thomas
" SHERIDAN, James
" SHERWIN, William Percival
Sgt. SIGG, Alfred Ernest
Pte. SIGLEY, James
" SILCOCK, Ernest Leonard
" SILLS, Reginald William
" SIM, Jack Lawrence
" SIMMONS, Albert
" SIMPSON, Alexander
Sgt. SIMPSON, Alfred Roy
L./Cpl. SIMPSON, George
Pte. SIMPSON, Joseph Alexander
" SIMPSON, John Francis
" SINCLAIR, Joseph Dunbar
L./Cpl. SKERMAN, Walter
" SKETCHLEY, William Patrick
Pte. SKEWES, Archer William
L./Cpl. SKINNER, Finlay
Pte. SKINNER, James
Driver SKUTHORPE, Claude
Pte. SLADE, Henry Charles
" SLATTER, Francis Thomas
" SMALL, David Joseph
L./Cpl. SMERDON, Francis
Pte. SMIDDY, William
L./Cpl. SMITH, Alexander
Pte. SMITH, Archie Bruce
" SMITH, Arthur George
Sgt. SMITH, Allen Hendy
Pte. SMITH, Albert Robert
" SMITH, Clarence Leslie, M.M.
" SMITH, Ernest
L./Cpl. SMITH, Ellis
Pte. SMITH, George
" SMITH, Gordon Vincent
" SMITH, Herbert Redcliffe, T.
" SMITH, James
" SMITH, John Joseph
" SMITH, John William
" SMITH, Phillip
" SMITH, Percival Alec
" SMITH, Samuel Gralton
" SMITH, Walter Herbert
" SMITH, William Shelton
" SMITHERAM, William Henry
" SMITON, Stuart
" SNELL, William George T.
" SNOW, Arthur
" SNOW Charles Sumner
Cpl. SOEGAARD, Alfred
Pte. SOMERVILLE, John
L./Sgt. SOORLEY, William Robert
Pte. SOROHAN, Harry William

Sgt. SPARROW, Stanley George
Pte. SPECHT, William
" SPENCER, Charles Lambert
" SPENCER, Ernest George
" SPENCER, Ernest William
" SPODE, Maurice Middlemore
" SPREEN, Robert
L./Cpl. SPRING, Harry
Pte. SPURLING, Richard Leslie
" STANFIELD, Francis
" STAPLETON, Albert, M.M.
" STARK, Frank Bell, M.M.
" STARKEY, Walter Weston
L./Cpl. STAUNTON, Matthew Bede
" STAFFORD, William Henry, M.M.
Pte. STEAD, Walter James
" STEEL, Jack
" STEELE, John
" STEEPER, Samual
" STEINHARDT, Henry Herbert
" STENZEL, Albert
" STEPHENS, Edward James
L./Cpl. STEPHENS, Harry Montague
Pte. STEPHENS, William
" STEPHENSON, Albert Edward
" STERNE, William John
Sgt. STEVENS, Eric Edwin
Pte. STEVENS, Frederick William
" STEVENS, James
" STEVENS, John Norman
" STEVENSON, John
" STEVENSON, Samuel
" STEWARD, Edward John
Pte. STEWARD, Walter William
L./Cpl. STEWART, Alexander Barnett
Sgt. STEWART, Charles Edward
Pte. STEWART, Francis
Sgt. STICHNOTH, Ferdinand August
Pte. STICKLEY, Sydney Richard
" STINSON, Stanley Frederick
" STIRRAT, John
" STOCKS, Clarence Henry
" STOKES, Roy James
" STONE, Isaac
" STOREN, John
" STORY, Lewis Ford
" STORY, Thomas John
" STOTT, Roy
" STRANDQUIST, Frederick James
" STREET, Charles Daniel P.
" STREETER, Alfred Hector
" STRINGER, Mason Claude K.
" STRIVENS, Horace
Cpl. STRONG, Clarence Henry

Pte. STROW, James
„ STRUGNELL, Alexander
Cpl. STUART, William Jack, M.M.
Pte. STUBBINGS, Edward
L./Cpl. STUBBS, Allan Foster
Pte. STUDT, Charles Frederick
„ SULLIVAN, Michael
„ SULLIVAN, Thomas Patrick
„ SUMMERS, Arthur Edward, M.M.
„ SURAWSKI, Thomas Jacob
Cpl. SUTTON, Horatio
Pte. SUTTON, William
„ SUTTON, William John
„ SVENSON, Wilfred
„ SWAN, Frederick James
Sgt. SWAN, Harold Webster
Pte. SWEENEY, Thomas Francis
„ SWEANEY, Jeremiah Erin
„ SWEENEY, Dennis
„ SVENSON, James William
„ SYKES, Francis Leslie
„ SYKES, Vincent Lewis
„ SYLVESTER, John Thomas
„ SYMONDS, Robert Hilary
„ TALLIS, Percy Norman
„ TALTY, Peter
„ TAME, Reginald John
„ TANWAN, Edwin Edgar
„ TANWAN, William
L./Cpl. TARDENT, Emile, M.M.
Pte. TAYLOR, James
„ TAYLOR, Leslie Arthur
„ TAYLOR, Walter Edgar
„ TAYLOR, William Leonard
„ TEYS, Donald
Cpl. THATCHER, Gledhill
Pte. THEE, Frederick John
L./Cpl. THISTLEWAITE, Leo Victor
Pte. THISTLEWAITE, William Arthur
„ THOMAS, Donald
„ THOMAS, Fred Albert
„ THOMAS, Gwilym Towers
„ THOMAS, Harry
„ THOMAS, Norman James K.
„ THOMAS, Vernon Edwin
„ THOMPSON, Alexander Munro
„ THOMPSON, David
„ THOMPSON, Eric, M.M.
„ THOMPSON, Francis Frederick
„ THOMPSON, George Raybould
„ THOMPSON, Harry
„ THOMPSON, James
Sgt. THOMPSON, John Ellis, M.M.
L./Cpl. THOMPSON, Robert Henry
Pte. THOMSEN, Colin, M.M.

Pte. THOMSON, John Samuel
L./Cpl. THOMSON, John Wilson
Pte. THORLEY, Charles David
L./Cpl. THORPE, John
Sgt. THOW, Clair Erqhart, M.M.
Pte. THUMPKINS, Percival Albert
„ THURESON, John Laves
„ TICKLE, Stanley Harvey
„ TIERNAN, Frank George
„ TILNEY, Charles Newton
L./Cpl. TILSTON, Edward Spencer
Pte. TOBLER, Herbert William
„ TOMLINSON, David Malcolm
„ TOMLINSON, Frederick
„ TOMLINSON, Robert Edward
„ TOOMEY, Arthur, M.M.
W.O. (2) TOOTH, Samuel William, D.C.M.
Pte. TOWELL, Alfred William
Cpl. TRACEY, Joseph
L./Cpl. TRATT, George
Sgt. TRAPP, John
Cpl. TRAVERS, Ernest Dudley
„ TREASURE, John Barker
Pte. TREMAYNE, John Henry
„ TRIBE, William John T.
„ TRONSON, Thomas Bleakley
„ TROY, Joseph Patrick
„ TRUASHEIM, Harold Phillip J.
„ TRUNDLE, Henry James
L./Cpl. TULK, Horatio
„ TUNKIN, William
Pte. TUNSTALL, Victor
„ TUPICOFF, Alexis
„ TURNER, Alfred
„ TURNER, John
„ TURNER, Victor John
„ TURNER, William Henry
„ TURTON, Harry
„ TUSKER, Albert
Cpl. TWEED, Cecil Darcy, M.M.
Pte. TWINING, Horace
L./Cpl. TYLER, George William
Pte. TYNAN, Michael Joseph
„ TYNAN, William
„ TYRRELL, John
„ TYSOE, Charles Henry
„ UNICOMB, Abram
„ UNWIN, Frederick
„ VALANTINE, William
L./Cpl. VALENTINE, Frank Walter
„ VALLINS, Herbert
Pte. VANCE, William Leonard
Cpl. VAUGHAN, Daniel Kevin
Sgt. VAUGHAN, Robert

N.C.O.'s AND OTHER RANKS DISCHARGED

Pte. VERE, George Percy M.
„ VESPERMAN, Leslie Hargrave
„ VIRGEN, Charles William
L./Cpl. VIRTUE, Jack Walter
Pte. WADSWORTH, Samuel
„ WAITE, Reginald
„ WAKEFIELD, William
„ WAKEFORD, George William
„ WALKER, Albert Robert
„ WALKER, Charles Gardiner
Sgt. WALKER, Ronald William, D.C.M.
Cpl. WALKER, Vivian
Pte. WALKER, Roy Stewart
Cpl. WALKER, William Francis
L./Cpl. WALKER, William George
Pte. WALLACE, Alfred Edwin D.
„ WALLACE, Norman
„ WALLACE, Robert
„ WALLACE, Robert John H.
Pte. WALLER, Horace Edwin
„ WALPOLE, Frederick Archer
L./Cpl. WALSH, John Michael
Pte. WALSH, Leonard Michael J.
„ WALSH, Richard James
„ WALSH, William Daniel
„ WALSH, Walter Patrick
„ WALTERS, Henry Bernard
„ WALTON, Eric
„ WALTON, Francis Mervyn
Sgt. WANSTALL, William James
Pte. WARD, Robert Andrew
„ WARD, William Frederick
L./Cpl. WARDROP, Robert Anderson
Pte. WARFIELD, Arthur
„ WARNICK, Esmond Andrew
„ WARR, Harry
„ WASLEY, John Henry
„ WATKINS, George Cecil
„ WATSON, Thomas
„ WATSON, Thomas Forsythe
„ WATSON, Walter Phillip
„ WATTS, Arthur John
„ WATTS, Harry Corder
L./Cpl. WATTS, Joseph Carlisle
Pte. WATTS, Roy Stewart
„ WEATHERALL, William Robert
„ WEATHERED, John Fenwick, M.M.
„ WEBB, Lewis Purnell
„ WEBB, Thomas Wilson
„ WEBB, William
„ WEBBER, Edwin
„ WEBBER, William Arnold
Cpl. WEBBER, William George

Sgt. WEBSTER, Joseph Walter, M.M.
Pte. WECKER, Frederick Charles
„ WEDDERICK, John Henry
„ WEEKS, Joseph
„ WELDON, William Henry
Cpl. WELLS, Alfred James
Sgt. WELLS, Richard
Pte. WELLS, William
„ WENDELIN, Claude Augustus
„ WERNER, Edward
„ WESTON, Leopold Horatio
„ WHEATLEY, Claude
„ WHEELER, Edward James
„ WHIP, Albert James
„ WHITCHER, Harry Thomas
„ WHITE, Charles
„ WHITE, George Henry
„ WHITE, Herbert Clarence
„ WHITE, John
„ WHITE, John Herbert
„ WHITE, John Joseph
„ WHITE, Raymond
„ WHITE, Robert
„ WHITE, Richard
„ WHITE, Walter John E.
„ WHITEFORD, Robert Daniel
L./Cpl. WHITEHEAD, Albert Edward
Sgt. WHITEHEAD, John Henry
Pte. WHITTAKER, George Albert
„ WHITTEN, James
„ WHITTRED, George William
„ WICKS, Harold
„ WICKS, Thomas Edwin
„ WIGHTMAN, James Johnston
„ WILCOX, Alan Gordon C.
L./Cpl. Driver WILKIN, Charles
Pte. WILKINS, Arthur
„ WILKINSON, John Francis
„ WILKINSON, Lance
„ WILLIAMS, George Hastings
Cpl. WILLIAMS, Humphrey Phillip
Pte. WILLIAMS, James Albert
Cpl. WILLIAMS, James Edwin
L./Cpl. WILLIAMS, Norman, M.M.
Pte. WILLIAMS, Percy Owen
„ WILLIAMS, Reuben
„ WILLIAMS, Stanley Arthur
„ WILLIAMSON, Alfred Edward
„ WILLIAMSON, George Henry
„ WILLS, John Henry, M.M.
„ WILMOT, William Arthur
Cpl. WILSON, Albert
Pte. WILSON, Albert
„ WILSON, David
„ WILSON, Frank, D.C.M.

Pte. WILSON, George William
Cpl. WILSON, Maurice Macintosh
Pte. WILSON, Thomas Norman
L./Cpl. WILSON, William Herbert
Pte. WILSON, William Stanley
„ WINCEN, Rupert Ernest
„ WINDOW, Walter
L./Cpl. WINGETT, Aubrey John
Pte. WINSTON, Albert
„ WINTER, Eric Leslie
„ WINTER, Leslie Sylvester
„ WINTER, Woodley
„ WINTERS, Stanley Robert
L./Cpl. WINZAR, Harry Samuel
R.S.M. WITHERWICK, Richard
Pte. WODE, William Charles
„ WOFF, William Lawrence
Cpl. WOOD, George Henry
Pte. WOOD, William
„ WOOD, William Anthony
„ WOODALL, John
Sgt. WOODMAN, Vivian Bernard
Pte. WOODWARD, George
„ WORGAN, John Wallace

Pte. WOTLEY, Hugh Wilfred
R.S.M. WRIGHT, Robert
Pte. WRIGHT, Thomas
„ WRIGHT, William, M.M.
„ WRIGHT, William
Driver WRIGLEY, Alfred Joseph
Pte. WYATT, John Edward B.
„ WYETH, Robert Arthur
„ WYLIE, Thomas
„ YARWOOD, Robert, M.M.
    (A.A.M.C. Attached)
„ YARWOOD, William
    (A.A.M.C. Attached)
„ YORKSTON, Thomas Forrest
„ YOUNG, Albert John M.
Cpl. YOUNG, John Alfred
Pte. YOUNG, Norman
„ YOUNG, Robert Soutter
„ YOUNG, Victor George
„ YOUNG, William Daniel
Sgt. YOUNGER, David Cherry
Pte. ZELLER, Richard
„ ZIMMERLE, Ernest William

SUPPLEMENTARY LIST

Pte. ADAMS, Charles
„ ALLEN, James John
„ ALLEN, William
„ BATCHELOR, Herbert
„ BERTWISTLE, Frederick Duncan
„ BIGGS, Herbert Henry
„ BINNIE, Archibald
„ BOWLES, Frederick
„ BRADFORD, George
„ BREEN, Jeffrey
„ BURNS, Henry Gavin
„ BURTON, Frederick George
Cpl. CAMPBELL, Edward Colin
Pte. CLIFFORD, William George
„ COLES, John William
„ COLLARD, Arthur Sydney
„ COMERFORD, John
„ COOK, Thomas
„ DALY, Patrick Joseph
„ DOIG, William Alexander
„ DUELL, Frederick George
„ DUNNE, Thomas

Pte. EDWARDS, George Edwin
„ ENGLAND, Harold William
„ FERGUS, Hugh
„ FLYNN, Oswald Hubert
„ FORSSELL, Algot Hall
„ FOWLER, Angus
„ FRANKOM, Dick Minchin
„ FRASER, William
„ FRASER, William Ambrose
„ FREEMAN-DURANTY, Guy
L./Cpl. GALLAGHER, John
Pte. GATES, William
„ GILL, George
„ GILMORE, John McLean
„ GLUYAS, John
„ GORDON, Edward James
„ GORDON, James
„ GORE, Frank Sidney
„ GRAY, George
„ HAACK, Joseph Christian G.
„ HALES, Ingram George
„ HANNAN, Denis Peter P.

Pte. HARRIS, George
„ HINDS, Alfred George
„ HIXON, Alfred William
„ HOSKIN, Richard
„ HOUSE, Jack
„ HOWARD, William
„ HUDSON, William Maybury
„ HUGHES, William
„ HULCOMBE, George
„ IRWIN, Thomas
„ JACKSON, Thomas David
„ JENKINS, Keith
„ JOHNSON, Charles
„ JOHNSON, John William
„ JORDAN, Harry
„ JULL, Alfred Ernest
„ JUSTO, Robert G.
„ KEATING, Alfred William D.
„ KENNEDY, John
„ KENNEDY, William Arthur
„ KERR, Alexander Lawrence
„ KITCHEN, Herbert
„ LEWIS, Sylvester
Sgt. LITTLE, Samuel Thomas
Pte. MACDONALD, Farquhar
„ MARLEY, William
„ MARSH, John Christopher
„ MARTIN, John
„ MARTIN, John James
„ MATTHEWS, James
„ MEMMOTT, Charles Frederick
„ MESSENGER, Arthur
„ MILES, Edward
„ MILLINGTON, Amos
„ McLENNAN, Arthur

Pte. McORCK, John
„ NYKVIST, Ernest Victor
„ O'KEEFE, Jeremiah
„ O'REILLY, Thomas Wilfred
„ PERRY, Maurice Gordon
„ PORTER, John
„ POWELL, Abraham
„ REID, Hugh Macfarlane
„ REMINGTON, Leslie Henry
„ RICHARDSON, George Alfred
„ ROSS, Joseph
Cpl. SCOTT, James Walter
Pte. SMITH, James Robert
„ SMITH, Wilfred Elphinstone
„ SMITH, Walter George
„ SPENCE, Charles Elton
„ STONE, Henry
„ SUMMERS, Ernest William
„ TATTERSALL, Thomas William
„ TAYLOR, John Westland
„ TAYLOR, Stanley Frederick
Pte. THOMPSON, John
„ THORPE, Edward Richard
„ TICHBORNE, Robert
„ TICKLE, Frank
„ TRACEY, Frederick Joseph
„ TUFFEE, Stanley Ewart
„ URQUHART, Alexander
„ WEBBER, William Richard
„ WILKINSON, Alexander
„ WILKINSON, Joseph
„ WILLS, Walter
„ WISHART, Alexander McCallum
„ WOOD, Albert

NON-COMMISSIONED OFFICERS AND OTHER RANKS KILLED IN ACTION, DIED OF WOUNDS OR SICKNESS

Pte. ADDISON, Arthur Alexander
„ ALCORN, Percy David
„ ALDERSON, Reginald
„ ALEXANDER, Laurence Christopher
„ ALFORD, George Henry
„ ALLEN, Daniel
„ ALLAN, Thomas
Sgt. ALLARD, Henry James, M.M.
Pte. ALM, Leslie Henrik B.
„ ANDERSON, Herbert James
„ ANSELL, Alfred Errold
„ ARMSTRONG, George
„ ARMSTRONG, James Ernest
„ ASPERY, Marcus Ward Henry
„ BAKER, Arthur Ernest Charles
„ BALDEY, Thomas Henry
„ BAKER, Ebenezer James
„ BARCLAY, James
„ BARNES, John
„ BARNETT, Sydney
„ BARRETT, Charles Richard
„ BARRETT, George Ernest
„ BARRY, Patrick
„ BARTON, Reginald
„ BARTRIM, Victor Macleay
„ BASING, Alfred Joseph
L./Cpl. BASSMAN, Albert Henry
Cpl. BATTERHAM, Herbert Thomas
Pte. BAUER, Henry
C.Q.M.S. BAXTER, Duncan
Pte. BAXTER, Harry
„ BEARMAN, Charles Henry
„ BEIRNE, Francis Joseph
„ BELLERT, William John
„ BENNETT, John Francis
„ BETTS, Francis Joseph
„ BICKERSTETH, Robert
Sgt. BISHOP, George
Cpl. BLACK, Adam Robert
Pte. BLACK, David Colin
L./Cpl. BONGERS, Frank Barton
Pte. BOWLES, Victor Henry
Sgt. BOWLING, James Leslie
Pte. BOWMAN, Walter Henry
Sgt. BRAITHWAITE, Thomas
Pte. BREWSTER, Edward Viro
„ BRIGGS, Charles

Pte. BROAD, David Allan
„ BROWN, Alick
„ BROWN, Charles Lambert
„ BROWN, Edward George
„ BROWN, Frederic
L./Cpl. BROWN, John Alexander
„ BROWN, William George, M.M.
Pte. BROWNING, Jack
„ BUCKLEY, John
„ BUDDEN, Joseph Frederick
„ BURTON, William Stephen
Cpl. BUTTERWORTH, Henry
Pte. BUSSON, Alfred
L./Cpl. CALVERT, Ernest
„ CAMPBELL, George Henry
Pte. CAREY, William Michael
„ CARLSON, David Fridengard
L./Cpl. CARMICHAEL, Archibald
Pte. CARNELL, William Robert
„ CARNEY, Frederick Norman
„ CARSELDINE, George Alfred
„ CATCHPOLE, John
„ CHADWICK, Frederick George
„ CHALKLEY, James Arthur
„ CHARLES, Bernard Wallace
„ CHIVERS, Albert Lawrence
„ CHREE, Harry
„ CHRISTENSEN, Victor
„ CLARE, Edward Vincent
„ CLARK, Edwin Charles
Sgt. COCKS, Harold Reginald
Pte. COLEMAN, Albert James
„ CONNELLY, Francis Joseph
„ COOK, Joseph Edwin
„ CORBETT, Leon Seymour
„ COSTELLO, Dominic John
L./Cpl. COSTIN, Harold Joseph
Pte. CROMPTON, John Henry
„ CUDDY, John
„ CUMMINS, Arthur Reginald
„ CUNNINGHAM, John William
„ CURRAN, Michael
„ CURRIE, Archibald
„ CURTIS, Wilfred
L./Cpl. DALEY, Michael John, M.M.
Pte. DANIEL, Harold Ernest
Driver DARCY, Patrick
Pte. DAVISON, William Hannand

N.C.O.'s AND OTHER RANKS DECEASED 159

L./Cpl. DECKHARDT, Robert
Pte. DEMPSEY, George
" DEVINE, Stephen Patrick
" De VIS, Leslie Holmes
" DOLGNER, Jack Frederick
" DONOVAN, Joseph William
" DOWN, George
" DOYLE, Richard Alexander
" DREDGE, John James
Sgt. DRISCOLL, Oswald James, M.S.M.
Pte. DUNN, Charles
" EAGER, Martin James
" EASLEA, Charles
Sgt. EASEMENT, Stuart Cecil
Pte. EASTWELL, Thomas Edward
" EATON, Herbert John
" ECCLESTON, Albert Ambrose
Sgt. EDGAR, Robert Douglas
Pte. EDWARDS, Richard George
" EIG, Frederick Charles
" ELLIOT, Thomas William
" ERNST, Lelia Lloyd
L./Cpl. EWING, Alexander
Pte. FALLON, John
" FERGUSON, Alexander
Cpl. FITTOCK, Edwin Rawlings
Pte. FLYNN, Michael Walter
" FLEMING, Reginald
" FLICK, Frederick Walter
" FLYNN, William
" FOOT, James Fitzroy
" FOX, John Thomas
" FRANKISH, Edwin Thomas
" FRANZ, Cecil Charles
" FRASER, Michael Arbuthnot
Sgt. FRITSCH, Martin Theodore
Pte. FRY, John Campbell
" GALL, Thomas
" GALLOWAY, Andrew
" GARRY, John Robert
" GAUL, Frederick
" GIBBONS, Wilfred Owen
" GILLIS, William
" GODBEE, David John
" GODDEN, Charles
Sgt. GOODE, Cyril Hazlewood
L./Cpl. GORRING, Stanley
Pte. GOULDING, Fred Raymond D.S.M.
" GOVERS, Wilford Horton
" GOWER, Ernest Alfred
" GRAF, Norman Dennis
" GRAY, Richard Henry
" GREEN, Frederick Joseph

Driver GREENBURY, Leslie Sydney
Pte. GREENBURY, Stanley (A.A.M.C. Attached)
L./Cpl. GREENFIELD, Harold
Pte. GREER, Stafford John
" GREEVY, Robert Herbert
" GREIG, Malcolm Murray
" GROOM, Littleton Campbell
L./Cpl. GWYNNE, Charles
Pte. HADEN, Ernest
" HALL, Edward
" HALL, Joe
" HALL, Roger Nicholson
" HALL, William Albert
L./Cpl. HALLAM, Morris William
Sgt. HANNAH, Walter William
Pte. HARLEY, Herbert William
L./Cpl. HARMS, Percy Edmond
Pte. HART, William James
" HARWOOD, William Malcolm
" HASTIE, Henry James
" HAWTHORNE, Walter Archibald
" HEAD, Edwin
Cpl. HECKSCHER, Benjamin Horace
Pte. HEDDLE, John Irvine
" HELION, James Joseph
L./Cpl. HILL, Ernest William
Pte. HILLYARD, Thomas Leonard
" HILTON, Leonard
" HINCHCLIFFE, Vincent Alexander
" HINDMARSH, Arthur Frederick
" HINDS, Edward Patrick, M.M.
" HOLDEN, Charles William
Cpl. HOLLEY, John Thomas
Pte. HOLLOWAY, Alfred Benjamin
" HOPES, Frederick William
" HOPP, Louis
" HORRIGAN, Cornelius
" HOSIER, Ernest
Driver HOWARD, Jesse
Pte. HUGHES, Arthur Ashton
" HULL, Horace
L./Cpl. HUME, John David
Pte. HUNTER, Thomas
" HUNTER, Thomas Paul
Cpl. HUNTINGTON, Francis Edric
Pte. HUTCHINSON, John Thomas
" IBBOTSON, Arthur Samuel
L./Cpl. JACOBSEN, Leslie Norman
Driver JAFFA, Horade Edward
Pte. JAMIESON, Andrew William
L./Cpl. JARRETT, Bernard Abrahem
Sgt. JOHANSEN, Charles Henry, M.M.

Pte. JOHNSON, Stewart William
Cpl. JOHNSTON, Andrew
„ JOHNSTON, David Lawrence
Pte. JOHNSTONE, Ernest Lytton
L./Cpl. JOHNSTONE, Alexander
Pte. JONES, Henry Walter
Cpl. JONES, Jonathon
Pte. KELLY, Edward Patrick
„ KELLY, Frank Alfred
„ KICKBUSH, Harry
„ KING, Arthur Charles
L./Cpl. KING, Albert Edward
Pte. KINNANE, John
„ KINNANE, Michael James
„ KINSEY, Willaim Roderick
„ KOSTER, William Frederick
„ KUPFER, Ernest
„ LAIRD, Finley
„ LAMB, Vivian Dawson
„ LAMBERT, Arthur Robert
„ LAMBERT, Urban Lewis
L./Cpl. LANE, Thomas Albion
Pte. LARRACY, James
„ LAURIE, George
„ LAURIE, William James
„ LEATHEM, James
„ LEACH, Frederick
„ LEESON, Walter Clarence
„ LENNON, James
„ LIGHTBODY, Peter James
„ LIMPUS, James Frederick
„ LITTLEBOY, George Thomas
„ LITZOW, Frederick Charles
„ LIVINGSTONE, Archibald
Cpl. LIVINGSTONE, Clifton Alwin
Pte. LONERGAN, Edward
Driver LONG, Henry
Pte. LOWTHER, Frank William
L./Cpl. LUSCOMBE, George Thomas
Pte. LYDON, Joseph Patrick
„ LYNAM, Timothy
„ MACGREGOR, John Macrae
„ MACKAY, Alec Auld
„ MACKAY, Reginald
L./Cpl. MACMILLAN, James
„ MACMILLAN, John Alexander
Pte. MADDERN, William Francis
„ MALONEY, Donald Joseph
„ MANCHESTER, Henry
Cpl. MANDERSON, Charles
Pte. MANDERSON, Thomas
L./Cpl. MARSH, Clarence Robert
Pte. MARSH, Reginald Howard
„ MARSHALL, Alban Edward
„ MARSHALL, Arthur Reid

L./Cpl. MARTIN, John
Sgt. MARTIN, Thomas Andrew
Pte. MASON, George Henry
„ MATHEWS, Patrick John
„ MATTHEWS, Robert
„ MAYS, Eric Walter
„ MEDHURST, Clarence
„ MEILING, John Alexander
„ MICHAEL, William
„ MIDDLETON, Arthur Leslie
L./Cpl. MILLAR, Ernest Albert
Pte. MILLENS, Edward James
L./Cpl. MILLER, David
Pte. MILLINGTON, Robert
„ MOON, Alexander Henry, M.M.
„ MOORE, Alfred
„ MOORE, Wilfred
„ MOORES, Francis
„ MORIARTY, Maurice
„ MORRALL, Robert Theodore
„ MORSE, Vernon Eustace
L./Cpl. MORTIMER, Stanley George
Cpl. MOYES, William Daniel
L./Cpl. MULLEN, William Henry
Pte. MULLER, George
„ MUNNICH, Henry William
L./Cpl. MUNRO, Robert, M.M.
Pte. MURRAY, William James
„ MUSKER, William Edward
Cpl. McBRIDE, Andrew Curry
Pte. McCARTHY, John
„ McCASKER, Charles Edward
Sgt. McCASKER, William Carr, M.M.
Pte. McCORMACK, Charles
Sgt. McCOWAN, Colin Douglas
Pte. McGREDDEN, John
Sgt. McCULLOUGH James Alexander
Pte. McDOWELL, John Kissock, M.M.
„ McGAGHAN, Thomas Joseph
„ McGRATH, Percy
„ McGREEVY, John Thomas
„ McINTYRE, Cecil Gladstone
„ McKAY, Francis Theodore
„ McLAREN, William Turnbull
„ McLENNAN, Peter Duncan
„ McMANUS, William Spencer
„ McMURTRIE, Alexander
„ McNEILL, George Andrew
„ McPHEE, John
Cpl. McVICAR, William
Pte. NASH, James Henry
L./Cpl. NASH, Nicholas Frank
C.Q.M.S. NEILSON, Frederick
Sorensen
Pte. NEWBIGGING, George

N.C.O.'s AND OTHER RANKS DECEASED

Pte. NEWLOVE, Eversen Wilsby
 „ NEWMAN, Arthur
 „ NICHOLSON, William James
 „ NICHOLSON, Lachlan Archibald
 „ NIGHTINGALE, William
Cpl. NIGRO, John
Pte. NOLAN, Herbert George
 „ NORRIS, Alexander
 „ O'DONOHUE, Thomas Joseph
 „ OLESEN, August
 „ ORR, Cuthbert Donald
Cpl. OSMOND, James Charles Edward
Pte. OWEN, Albert George
 „ OWENS, Jack
 „ PARRY, George Edwin
 „ PARSONS, Thomas Henry
 „ PASCOE, Harry
 „ PATERSON, Stanley Richard
L./Cpl. PATTISON, Arthur
Cpl. PAYNE, Arthur John
L./Cpl. PAYNE, Charles Richard
Pte. PAYNE, John
 „ PEARCE, Edward Charles
 „ PEET, William James
 „ PERKINS, Harry
 „ PERRO, Thomas Kerr
 „ PEWTER, Arthur
 „ PHILLIPS, George Frederick
 „ PITT, Joseph
 „ PITTS, Daniel John
 „ POULTON, George Henry
 „ POWER, William Thomas Galvin
 „ PRICE, Owen Bennion
 „ PROUT, Arthur
 „ PURSER, Charles Glenroy
Cpl. RALEIGH, James Alexander
Pte. RAND, Oliver George
 „ RANGER, Raymond Leslie
 „ RAWLINGS, Ernest John
Cpl. RAWLINSON, Taylor
Pte. RAYBOURNE, William Ross
 „ REDPATH, George
 „ REID, Benjamin
L./Cpl. RHODES, Grafton Edward
Pte. RICHARDS, Arthur Victor
 „ RICHARDS, Lindsay Gordon
 „ RICHARDSON, James Daniel
 „ RICHARDSON, Robert Charles George
Pte. ROBB, John
 „ ROBERTS, Oswald Warwick
L./Cpl. ROGER, Alexander
Pte. ROLLINSON, Herbert Thomas
 „ ROWBOTHAM, Arthur Francis
 „ ROWLANDS, Charles Edward

Pte. RUFF, Charles William
 „ SANDFORD, William Frederick
 „ SANDS, Alfred Henry
 „ SCANLAN, Patrick William
 „ SCANLAN, John
 „ SCOLYER, Frank Harold
 „ SCOTT, Edward
L./Cpl. SCOTT, Harold
Pte. SEYMOUR, Francis Douglas
Cpl. SHANKS, William, M.M.
Pte. SHEPHERDSON, Fanrk Stanley
 „ SHERRAS, Jack William
 „ SHOOTER, Harold Albert
 „ SHORT, Walter Thomas
 „ SINCLAIR, William Henry
 „ SKINNER, Samuel Henry
 „ SMITH, Albert Gilbert
 „ SMITH, John Henry
 „ SMITH, John Livingston
 „ SMITH, Percy James
 „ SNOW, Frederick Robert
L./Cpl. SORRENSEN, Leslie Andrew
Sgt. STEEL, William
Pte. STEPHENS, Lindsay Gordon
 „ STEVENSON, William James
 „ STEWART, Robert
 „ STOCKWELL, Charles
 „ SULLIVAN, William Patrick
L./Cpl. SUMMERS, James Stanley
Pte. SUTHERS, John
Pte. SUTTON, Joseph Reginald
 „ TANNER, Allan Harcourt
 „ TARDENT, Edward Felix
 „ TAYLOR, Edward John
Sgt. TAYLOR, Hubert Lancelot
Pte. TAYLOR, William James
 „ THISTLEWAITE, Albert Elihu
 „ THOMAS, John
 „ THOMAS, Phillip Lewis
 „ TUCKEY, Claude Wilfred Bourne
 „ TURNER, Harold
 „ TURNER, Sydney
 „ TUZZI, Francis
L./Cpl. TWEED, Herbert William
Pte. TWIGG, Arthur Reid
Cpl. TYACK, Sydney
L./Cpl. WAKELY, John Charles
Pte. WALTERS, Herbert Stanley
 „ WALTON, John
 „ WARD, Albert
 „ WARD, Sidney Collins
 „ WARREN, Henry John
 „ WATSON, Arriness Herbert
 „ WATSON, John
 „ WATSON, William George, M.M.

Pte. WEBB, Harry
„ WEBBER, John Manley
Sgt. WEST, Charles Herbert
Pte. WESTWOOD, Eric Joseph
Sgt. WHEELDON, Alston Lyle
Pte. WHELAN, Maurice Vincent
„ WHITE, Benjamin David
„ WHITE, Frederick George Woodbine
„ WHITE, Harold Sydney
„ WILKINSON, Bert
Pte. WILLIAMS, John
„ WILLIAMS, Jack
„ WILLIAMS, Norman Alexander

W.O. WILSON, Stanley, D.C.M.
Pte. WINTHORP, Neville Everleigh
„ WINKS, Clinton James Nicholson M.M.
„ WISE, Frank William
„ WITTE, Henry Llewellyn
Cpl. WOOD, Francis George
Pte. WOODS, Thomas Desmond
„ WRIDE, Leslie Percy
Cpl. WYNNE, Floyd Owen Robert
Pte. YATES, Edward
„ YEOMAN, Albert
„ YOUNG, Claverhouse
„ YOUNG, George

Decorations Awarded 42nd Battalion, A.I.F.

Pte. ADAM AITKEN, M.M.
For bravery in the Field.

L./Sgt THOMAS HENRY ALEXANDER, C. de G. (Belgian).
For conspicuous services rendered in the Field.

Lieut. WILLIAM EWART ALLAN, M.C.
On the 4th April, 1918, during enemy attacks along the south bank of the Somme, when the Battalion on our right had fallen back, Lt. Allan went across the Somme, and, while the retirement was in progress, he moved about among the troops rallying them, and as soon as the possibility of consolidation was decided upon he sent off most excellent and accurate information of the situation to Battalion Headquarters. He then moved along the line and established the location of the whole Battalion line, and throughout was constantly subjected to heavy fire from enemy machine-guns and snipers. This officer has, since arriving in the line on 27th March, 1918, behaved with great gallantry. On the night of attack on Sailly Laurette, his patrol duty, and his work as liaison officer under fire was exceptionally good. Without doubt it was due to the personal effort and devotion to duty of this officer that the right flank of the 42nd Battalion was made secure on the occasion in question.

Sgt. HENRY JOHN ALLARD, M.M.
On the 31st July in the assault East of Messines, this man displayed great initiative and cool courage. On his Platoon Commander becoming a casualty, he took charge of the platoon and reorganised it under heavy machine-gun fire. After the assault he successfully withdrew his men and started them on their allotted tasks of digging communication trenches. His coolness and energy afforded an excellent example to the men and contributed largely to our success on this sector.

Cpl. NORMAN ANDREW, M.M.
During the period from the 3rd to the 10th July inclusive when his Battalion was in the trenches in the Messines Section, this man was in charge of ration waggons returning from White Spot Cottage on the night 9th/10th July, 1917. Whilst coming down the track from Messines Ridge heavy enemy gunfire opened upon the track, resulting in one driver being wounded, one mule killed, and one mule injured. It was then that this man showed great courage and coolness, although shells were falling around the spot continuously, he dressed the wounds

of the Driver, and got him into safety in a dug-out. He then returned to the scene of the accident and cleared the track of the wagon and dead mule, thereby saving a serious congestion of traffic. He had on previous occasions shown great coolness and courage in getting drivers and waggons through serious trouble.

Pte. FRANK HERBERT ATTRIDGE, M.M., M.I.D.

On 29th September, 1918, during operations south of Bony, private Attridge, who was employed as Company Runner, was sent with several messages to platoons, and other units on the flanks and on the front. On each occasion he had to go through extremely heavy enemy machine-gun and shell fire. The night was also very wet and pitch dark, but Private Attridge successfully carried out his work. When his platoon became detached from the remainder of the company he volunteered to go out and find them, which he did, and guided them back under heavy enemy fire. During the whole operation his splendid bearing and devotion to duty set a great example to his comrades. M.I.D. for conspicuous services rendered.

Lieut. LESLIE WALTER BARNES, M.C.

For conspicuous gallantry and devotion to duty when in command of his platoon in an attack, and of the company after all the other officers became casualties. He carried out the work of consolidation under adverse weather conditions and heavy enemy barrages.

Sgt. JOHN BARNETT, M.M.

On the night of the 5th/6th June, in the trenches near Hill 63, this N.C.O. was a member of a raiding party against the enemy trenches. Under his Officer (Second Lieut. Price) he led the assault, which was pushed home with such vigour that the demoralised enemy garrison cast down their arms and fled through our barrage. Corporal Barnett displayed great coolness and courage by pushing out in advance of the assaulting party in an endeavour to capture a prisoner. Being unable to overtake the enemy, he knelt in the open and developed a rapid rifle fire that was seen to inflict casualties on the fleeing enemy. On withdrawing from the enemy lines Corporal Barnett again displayed great coolness in assisting a wounded comrade back. He was the last of the party to enter our lines. His coolness, initiative and bravery set a stimulating example to the remaining members of the raiding party. A total of 5 officers and 100 men took part in this raid.

W.O. JOHN HENNESSY BAYNES, M.S.M.

For continuous good service and devotion to duty. R.Q.M.S. Baynes has rendered excellent and efficient service since November, 1916, and it is largely due to the energetic and efficient manner in which he handles his work that the men of the Battalion have at all times been well cared for under conditions of trench warfare, when in rest, and during recent operations for the past three months on the Somme. During the absence of the Quartermaster, the responsibility for this department has rested upon R.Q.M.S. Baynes, and he has often displayed his ability to handle supply matters in any emergency.

Pte. GRAHAM BELL, M.M.

On 29/9/18 during operations south of Bony, Private Bell did excellent work as a Company Runner when the company was engaged mopping up the Hindenburg Line. On the evening of the 29/9/18 he had to pass through a very heavy machine-gun barrage no less than three different times, carrying messages from the front line to the support line. As the messages were very urgent, he had to make his runs over the top of the ground, as going through the Communication Trench which was some distance away, would take too long. In the early morning of the 30/9/18 he again did excellent work in carrying messages to advanced Battalion H.Q. under heavy enemy artillery fire. Owing to Private Bell's devotion to duty and promptness in delivering messages several enemy strong points were overcome.

Cpl. REGINALD ROBERT BELL, M.M.
For bravery in the Field.

Pte. ROY BENTLEY, M.M.
For bravery in the Field.

Sgt. FREDERICK DAVID BIRKETT, C. de G. (Belgian).
For conspicuous services rendered.

Lieut. ARTHUR CHARLES BOORMAN, M.C.
On the 12th August, 1918, during operations on the Somme, near Proyart, this officer showed great coolness and command under trying circumstances. After reaching the final objective his platoon was suffering casualties from enemy machine-gun fire; taking three men he rushed the post, drove the enemy out and inflicted heavy casualties. Later when the enemy was strongly reinforced he successfully manoeuvred his platoon and established them in a stronger position without a casualty. Throughout the whole attack he showed splendid courage and devotion to duty. This officer also handled his platoon during the attack East of Hamel on the 8th August, in a most satisfactory manner. By his absolute control he was able to manoeuvre his platoon against the enemy and his promptness of action at times very materially assisted the advance.

Company Q.M.S. JAMES BREBNER, M.I.D.
For conspicuous services rendered.

Pte. JAMES FREDERICK BRIGHT, M.M.
For bravery in the Field

L./Cpl. WILLIAM BROWN, M.M.
For bravery in the Field.

Cpl. GEORGE LOVE BROWN (Attached A.A.M.C.), M.M.
For bravery in the Field.

Pte. CHARLES FRANCIS BUTLER, M.M.
For conspicuous devotion to duty during the period 16th September, 1918, to 11th November, 1918. During the period Private Butler was acting as a Company Runner, and was thus exposed to very heavy enemy fire. He never failed to deliver messages, and his courage and devotion to duty was a fine example to all.

Pte. WALTER JAMES BRYANT, M.M.

At 1 p.m. on 30th March, 1918, near Sailly le Sec, Private Walter James Bryant noticed a runner carrying a despatch to the front line, fall under the fire of heavy artillery and machine-guns. He at once leaped from his trench and obtained the message from the wounded man and delivered it to the Company Commander in the front line. This action was responsible for the rapid delivery of an important message, and was carried out with the utmost coolness and conspicuous bravery under heavy fire from artillery and machine-guns. By his prompt and brave action he not only set a fine example to all other men around him, but delivered promptly a message that was of urgent importance for the tactical employment of the troops holding the line.

Major COLIN CLYDE CAMPBELL, M.B.E.

For conspicuous services rendered.

Sgt. ROBERT AUBREY FRASER CAMPBELL, D.C.M.

For conspicuous gallantry and devotion to duty. He led his platoon with great success in an attack and handled it with splendid skill under difficult conditions. He assisted in capturing an enemy machine-gun with its crew. He sent back valuable and timely information, and contributed to the success of the operation by his courage and leadership.

Pte. WILLIAM JOHN CHADWICK, M.M.

On 29th September, 1918, during operations south of Bony, Private Chadwick, as No. 2 of a Lewis Gun which had been mounted on the parapet to put a hostile machine-gun out of action, kept the Lewis Gun supplied with magazines while under fire from at least five enemy machine-guns until the hostile gun was put out of action. Later in the day Private Chadwick observed an enemy party working down a communication trench. Taking his Lewis Gun he brought fire to bear on them. Under very heavy machine gun fire he covered the advance of our bombers who succeeded in clearing the trench. His courage and coolness prevented a strong party of the enemy from reaching our trench.

Pte. WILLIAM COCKSHUTT, M.M.

On the 12th August, 1918, during the operations on the Somme near Proyart this man did splendid work when assisting with others to capture a machine gun position. He threw bombs and attracted the attention of the enemy whilst our Lewis Gun moved into position, and as soon as it opened fire he rushed the enemy post and killed one of the gunners, the remainder being forced to surrender. The No. 1 of the Lewis gun having become a casualty, Private Cockshutt took the gun and continued the advance.

Cpl. ROBERT COOK, M.M.

For bravery and devotion to duty. On the 4th July, 1918, during the attack on Hamel, Corporal Cook displayed great gallantry and initiative in using his Lewis gun under heavy enemy fire. During the assault on the final position, where the enemy were in large numbers, this N.C.O. rushed forward with his Lewis gun and opened fire on the enemy trench, thus enabling the other members of his platoon to rush the position with a minimum of casualties. During the whole operation Corporal Cook showed conspicuous courage and devotion to duty.

Pte. ALBERT COOPER, M.M.
: For bravery in the Field.

Cpl. STANLEY CORBETT, M.M.
: For bravery in the Field.

Cpl. WILLIAM JOSEPH CORRY, M.M.
: For bravery in the Field.

Sgt. ROBERT JOHNSTON CROWE, M.M.
: For bravery in the Field.

L./Cpl. MICHAEL JOHN DALEY, M.M.
: On the 4th July, 1918, during the attack on Hamel, L./Cpl. Daley showed exceptional skill and bravery in leading his section to the attack. During the final assault an enemy machine-gun temporarily held up his section. Daley promptly rushed forward under cover of Lewis gun fire, bombed the gun and killed the crew, thus enabling the final position to be carried. Throughout the whole operation L./Cpl. Daley showed untiring devotion to duty and set a splendid example to the men of his section.

Sgt. NORMAN WESLEY DANIEL, M.M.
: For bravery in the Field.

Cpl. PHILIP SPENCER DAY, M.M.
: On the 8/8/18 during operations on the Somme, east of Hamel, this N.C.O. displayed great gallantry, organising power, and initiative. In spite of the heavy machine-gun fire against his platoon, he fought his way to the objective through the dense fog, keeping good communication throughout the advance and inflicting heavy losses on the enemy. His platoon reached its objective without casualties and properly organised.

Major EDWARD JOHN DIBDIN, D.S.O., M.I.D.
: For distinguished service during the period February 25th to September, 1918. Major Dibdin commanded the 42nd Battalion with great skill and initiative during the attack on Hamel on July 4th, 1918. On the 8th and 12th August he again skilfully commanded the 42nd Battalion with great drive and energy, attaining all his objectives. He commanded the 41st Battalion from the 31st August to 9th September, during the advance from Mont St. Quentin to Roisel with marked success. M.I.D. for conspicuous services rendered.

Lieut. VICTOR CHARLES DIXON, D.C.M.
: For conspicuous gallantry and devotion to duty. When his platoon commander and N.C.O.'s had become casualties, he immediately organised a platoon and led them to the assault of enemy posts, which he captured and consolidated with the utmost skill and good judgment. His conduct and his skilful handling proved a great stimulus to all his men, both during the assault and when under heavy artillery fire, during the whole of which time he displayed a total disregard of danger.

Sgt. CYRIL DONKIN, M.M.

For bravery in the Field.

Gunner SAMUEL JOHN DREW, M.M.

On 24th April, 1918, between the junction of the rivers Somme and Ancre, a/Bdr. Drew was in charge of the telephonists of the Battery. During the enemy's bombardment of gas and H.E., which lasted eight hours, a/Bdr. Drew, in company with Gnr. Ridgeway, worked continuously on the telephone lines, and under tremendous difficulties, got in touch with group headquarters. The lines were broken by hostile shell fire continuously, and these men displayed the greatest courage and ability spending practically the whole day on the lines, exposed throughout to incessant and heavy shell fire. Both performed splendid work, showing complete disregard for personal safety.
(Won with 28th Battery, 8th Australian Field Artillery).

Sgt. OSWALD JAMES DRISCOLL, M.S.M.

Sgt. O. J. Driscoll, has been Transport Sergeant since the formation of the Transport Section, and has always carried out his work with utmost enthusiasm and devotion to duty. During operations at Messines, Warneton, and Ypres, his work was exceptionally satisfactory, and carried out under very adverse conditions and at great risk. It was due to his grit and determination that the supply of rations and ammunition were successfully delivered to the men of this Battalion in the line on October 4th and 10th near Passchendale.

Captain GORDON ALLAN DUNBAR, M.C., C. de G. (Belgian), M.I.D.

For consistent good work and gallantry in action during the last Somme operations in 1918 as Regimental Adjutant, and as acting G.S.O. on Divisional Headquarters. In carrying out his duties under fire, Captain Dunbar has shown cool judgment and gallantry of a high order in every way equal to the reputation he gained as a Company Commander. His services as Adjutant were invaluable to the 42nd Battalion in action whilst the accuracy and quickness of his reports were of the greatest assistance to the Divisional Staff. C. de G., for conspicuous services rendered in the Field. M.I.D. for conspicuous services rendered.

Pte. TIMOTHY JOSEPH DWYER, M.M.

For bravery in the Field.

Pte. WILLIAM FREDERICK EISING, M.M.

On 29th September, 1918, during operations south of Bony, Private Eising was employed as a Company Runner. When the company was going forward he was sent back to Battalion Headquarters with despatches, and also to guide the ration mules up to the companies. He had to go through exceptionally heavy shell fire and over difficult and strange country in intense darkness and heavy rain. He delivered the message and returned with the ration. He then volunteered to guide the ration parties to each company under heavy shell fire, for which he showed utter disregard. By this splendid bearing he set a great example of courage and devotion to duty to all ranks.

DECORATIONS AWARDED THE FORTY-SECOND 169

L./Sgt. WILLIAM FAHEY, M.M., Bar to M.M.

On 1/9/18, during operation north of Peronne, when his Platoon Commander and all Platoon N.C.O.'s had become casualties Private Fahey assumed command and carried on with great dash and initiative. He led his platoon to the correct line of the objective, and whilst there displayed great coolness and command of his men in spite of heavy enemy barrage fire. He made intelligent use of all ground and kept up communication with his Company ·Commander in a manner worthy of the highest praise. Bar to M.M.: On 29th September, 1918, during operations South of Bony, Corporal Fahey did splendid work with his section in clearing up obscure situations and patrolling. When the company had to move forward to a new line he was mainly responsible for obtaining touch with the troops on the flank. Corporal Fahey and his section later went out in face of heavy artillery and machine-gun fire and did splendid work in reporting and sending back valuable information as to the position in front. His task was made very difficult as it was daylight, and nothing was known as to the whereabouts of the enemy in front. His coolness and courage throughout the operation was of the highest order.

Lieut. GEORGE BYERLEY FORSTER, M.M., Bar to M.M.

On 8/8/18 during the operations on the Somme, East of Hamel, Sergeant Forster kept well forward of his platoon during the whole of the advance, cleaned up several dug-outs singlehanded and captured a number of prisoners. On reaching the objective he immediately set in position two enemy machine-guns which his platoon used to great advantage in keeping down the enemy's fire during consolidation and also materially assisting the advance of the 4th Australian Division. His courage and absolute disregard for his personal safety, combined with his skilful leadership, set a high example to all ranks under his command. Bar to M.M.: On 29/9/18, during operations South of Bony, when the situation was obscure, Sergeant Forster volunteered on three different occasions under heavy machine-gun fire to patrol and get in touch with neighbouring units. Once when the patrol was scattered by heavy artillery fire, he showed great coolness and leadership in reorganising his men and succeeded in getting in touch with the foremost troops of another Battalion, who were then within 40 yards of the enemy and engaged in a bombing fight. On night 1-2/10/18 his company was ordered to take up a new position, Sergeant Forster who had been over the route once, volunteered and guided the company over very difficult ground covered with shell holes and wire, to a new position in the quickest possible time, despite the fact that the night was extremely dark and heavy rain was falling. Throughout the operations Sergeant Forster showed keenness and reliability and resource of the highest order.

Pte. RICHARD ALBERT FERGUSON, M.M.

On the 8/8/18, during the operations on the Somme, east of Hamel, Private Ferguson rendered valuable assistance as a runner, carrying and delivering many messages through enemy shell fire and machine-gun fire, and over bad ground, without hesitation. The success which the platoon had in reaching the objective without being disorganised in spite of the dense fog and the bad ground, was chiefly due to Private Ferguson for the manner in which he assisted his platoon commander in keeping touch among the sections. Throughout the whole operation he was indefatigable in rendering help possible, thereby setting a high example of devotion to duty.

Lieut. ROBERT DAVID FISHER, M.C.
For distinguished service in the Field.

Lieut. GEORGE FRANKHAM, M.M., M.I.D.
On the 8/8/18, during the operations on the Somme Sergeant Frankham did splendid work and showed skilful leadership as a platoon Sergeant. He advanced his platoon rapidly in spite of the difficulties arising from dense fog and thick growth of underbush. During the advance on the objective he showed unflinching courage in personally mopping up dug-outs and taking prisoners. On reaching the objective, he at once consolidated and established a Lewis Gun Post, on a bridge, cleared up all surrounding ground and succeeded in capturing more prisoners. He also kept good liaison with the platoon on the north bank of the Somme. Throughout the operations Sergeant Frankham's splendid leadership and exemplary courage was excellent example to all ranks. M.I.D. for conspicuous services rendered.

Pte. RICHARD GILLESPIE, M.M.
For bravery in the Field.

Lieut. HUGH EDWARD GILMOUR, M.M.
During the period from the 3rd to the 10th July inclusive, when his Battalion was in the trenches in the Messines Sector, Sergeant Gilmour displayed great courage and devotion to duty. On the nights 4-5/7/17 he was in charge of a party which established and consolidated a post in the vicinity of two enemy strong points. By vigorous offensive action he caused these points to be evacuated and on the night of 6-7th July, he again led his section forward and established another post within 50 yards of the enemy's line of consolidation. On the night of 8-9/7/17 he successfully defended the post against a hostile enterprise. During the whole of this work he continually passed through heavy enemy machine-gun fire while laying out tests and carrying forward rations pending the construction of communication trenches. This N.C.O.'s coolness and courage throughout inspired his men with the greatest confidence, and his fine example of devotion to duty was chiefly instrumental in gaining ground from the enemy, and establishing our line in a good tactical position.

L./Cpl. WILLIAM ALBERT GOODLAND, M.M.
On the 8/8/18 during the operations on the Somme, east of Hamel, Private Goodland showed conspicuous bravery in rushing an enemy trench single-handed, where he killed some of the enemy who refused to surrender, and captured several prisoners. He set a high example throughout the operation of personal courage and devotion to duty.

Pte. FRED RAYMOND GOULDING, D.C.M.
For conspicuous gallantry and devotion to duty whilst acting as a Company Runner. Four times he successfully carried messages through a heavy barrage from an isolated portion of the line, a distance of half a mile, on the last occasion returning exhausted and shaken by an explosion. In spite of this he volunteered to take another message and through his wonderful courage and determination his battalion was able to deal successfully with a difficult situation.

DECORATIONS AWARDED THE FORTY-SECOND

Sgt. EDGAR RICHARD GRAHAM, M.M.

On the 8/8/18 during the operations on the Somme, east of Hamel, Sergeant Graham took command of his platoon when his Platoon Commander became a casualty, and in spite of heavy enemy fire and dense fog he kept his men well under command, reaching the objective with his platoon complete in numbers. Throughout the whole operation he set a fine example of courage and initiative which inspired all ranks to do their utmost.

Sgt. HENRY GREER, D.C.M.

On the 8th August, 1918, during the operations on the Somme, Sergeant Greer's Platoon Commander became a casualty. This N.C.O. immediately took command of the platoon, and, with a small party of men, he cleared up two large dugouts, taking in all about 50 prisoners. On reaching the objective, in spite of heavy enemy machine-gun fire, he personally established a forward post. Throughout the operations he showed consummate skill in leadership and organisation, and inspired all by his untiring devotion to duty.

Pte. WILLIAM LEWIS GRENDON, M.M.

For bravery in the Field.

Lieut. WALTER CHARLES HAGGETT, M.M.

On the 31st July, 1917, East of Warneton—Gapaard Road—this N.C.O. displayed great courage and devotion to duty throughout the action. His Platoon Commander became a casualty during the assault on the first objective and this N.C.O. assumed charge and led them on to the final objective, which was only wrested from the enemy after a vigorous hand to hand engagement. During this conflict he displayed great courage and his party inflicted severe casualties on the enemy. His conduct throughout the assault and during the consolidation under heavy artillery and machine-gun fire was excellent.

Cpt. ALBERT EDWARD HALSTEAD, M.C.

On the 4th October, 1917, during the Broodseinde attack, Captain A. E. Halstead, was in command of D Company, 42nd Battalion. On gaining the objective for the Battalion, touch had been lost with the Battalion, on the left. This officer had his flank considerably extended in this direction, and during the supervision of the movement, showed utter disregard for danger from enemy snipers, artillery, and machine-gun fire. When attempting to locate an active machine-gun, he approached a pill-box alone and obtained seven prisoners. His action throughout the whole attack was marked with the same disregard for personal danger. On the 31st July, 1917, during the Warneton attack, this officer controlled his company in attack and consolidation with great skill and courage, and at great personal risk. His administration and control have been of a highly satisfactory standard since the commencement of operations in December, 1916, since when he has been continually with the Battalion.

Pte. JOHN HARE, M.M.

On the 11th and 12th August, 1918, during the operations on the Somme near Proyart, this man was employed as a runner to forward battalions, and although badly shaken by the explosion of an enemy bomb during the night, he refused to leave his duty. On many of his journeys he had to pass through heavy enemy barrage of shell and machine-gun fire and succeeded in delivering and bringing valuable information which was essential to the success of the operation. He also distinguished himself in this duty during the attack East of Hamel on the 8/8/18, and his courageous actions and splendid spirit showed a fine sense of duty to the remainder of his comrades.

L./Sgt. EDGAR ERNEST HARMAN, M.M., Bar to M.M.

At Armentieres, on 1/2/17, was in charge of scouts working with a raiding party of his Battalion. On returning to our lines at daybreak, when the raid was over, he learned that one of the party was missing. He at once returned to "No-man's Land," and assisted Lieut. May in bringing in the body of Private Wise. He afterwards searched "No-man's Land" and succeeded in bringing in the Lewis gun which Private Wise had been using. During the whole period he was subjected to heavy fire from machine-guns which were working with the aid of a searchlight. Bar to M.M.: On the 8th August, 1918, during the operations on the Somme, East of Hamel this N.C.O. gave valuable assistance to the scout officer in laying assembly tapes, cutting the wire, and guiding the Battalion to assembly positions. Having previously had a knowledge of an enemy strong post, as soon as the barrage lifted he, in company with an officer, rushed the post and captured 24 of the enemy, including an officer and a machine-gun. Throughout the operation this N.C.O. showed a very high example of courage and devotion to duty.

Sgt. CHARLES FREDERICK WILLIAM HARRIS, M.M.

For bravery in the Field.

Cpl. WILLIAM HASKINS, M.M.

On the 12th August, 1918, during operations on the Somme when the Battalion was advancing on Proyart Ridge this man was severely wounded, and after having the wound dressed he continued the advance but was immediately wounded again. After receiving further attention he advanced with his company until blown over with a shell. He continued to advance with the remainder of another platoon, and engaged enemy machine-gun with rifle fire. Stretcher-bearers being wounded he volunteered to carry out a very heavy man, and did so under intense machine-gun and ground shrapnel fire, bringing the wounded man 2½ kilos to the R.A.P.

Pte. EDWARD PATRICK HINDS, M.M.

For bravery in the Field.

L./Cpl. THOMAS LEONARD HOLLOWAY, D.C.M.

For conspicuous gallantry and devotion to duty when in charge of a Lewis gun section. When his officer was wounded, he led his platoon with great dash and determination, overcoming all opposition and inflicting heavy casualties on the enemy. With his Lewis gun he dispersed a hostile counter-attack, and, by the courage and initiative which he displayed until he was severely wounded, very largely contributed to the defeat of the enemy.

Cpl. JAMES HUTCHINSON, M.M.

On 8/8/18, during the operation on the Somme, this N.C.O. kept his platoon well organised and well in hand. In spite of the dense fog and heavy enemy shell fire during the advance, this N.C.O. kept up good communication between flank units. His platoon reached its objective properly organised and with numbers complete and captured during the fight 27 prisoners besides inflicting numerous casualties on the enemy. Throughout the operation he set a fine example of courage and initiative.

Lieut. THOMAS JACK, M.C.

For conspicuous gallantry and devotion to duty. Although he had been twice buried by shell fire, he proceeded through an intense hostile barrage to the front line, which had been temporarily thrown into confusion, and at once reorganised the line under very great difficulties and at great personal risk. By his excellent example he restored the morale of the front line troops, and undoubtedly saved many lives.

Pte. ANDREW JAKEMAN, M.S.M.

On the 4th/5th October, 1917, during operations at Zonnebeke, Private Andrew Jakeman, Runner, for 48 consecutive hours carried messages from the front line to Battalion Headquarters through heavy enemy shell fire, rain and mud, without sleep or rest. After this period, although practically exhausted, he gallantly volunteered to take the place of a comrade who was put out of action by shell shock, and continued to carry messages. On one occasion he carried an extremely urgent message through a hurricane barrage without hesitation. This man also displayed great courage as a guide during gas bombardments at Messines, and carrying a wounded officer during Warneton operations through a heavy barrage to safety. The spontaneity of response to any call for duty from this man, his courage and devotion to duty, are worthy of the reward that has been submitted.

Sgt. CHARLES HENRY JOHANSEN, M.M.

For bravery in the Field.

L./Cpl. GERVAISE ESDAILE JOLLY, C. de G. (Belgian).

For conspicuous services rendered in the Field.

T./W.O. 1. WLLIAM JAMES JUDD, M.M.

On the morning of July 31st, 1917, in the assault North of Warneton, this N.C.O. was wounded shortly after leaving our own trenches. He took charge of the platoon and with them, mopped up enemy strong posts. He then re-organised his men, led them successfully to their objective, and did not leave them to have his wound dressed until he had placed them all on their tasks. His courage and devotion to duty were a fine example to the platoon.

Sgt. JOSEPH KEARNEY, M.I.D.

For conspicuous services rendered.

Sgt. EDWIN LANG KELLY, M.S.M.
For meritorious service and devotion to duty during the period 25th February and 17th September, 1918. This N.C.O. has performed the duties of Battalion Orderly Room Sergeant in an exemplary manner, and has been of great assistance to the Adjutant in relieving him of much of the administrative work during operations when the Adjutant was otherwise engaged. On the 24th April at Bonney, when the village was being heavily shelled with gas and H.E., Sergeant Kelly personally packed up and ensured the safe custody of valuable records and papers of the Battalion.

Pte. WILLIAM JOHN KIM, M.M.
On 31st July, 1917, East of Warneton-Gapaard—this man showed great bravery during the action against enemy strong points. He was mainly responsible for the rapid evacuation of wounded up till 8 p.m., when he himself became a casualty. His absolute disregard for machine-gun and shell fire in carrying out his duties as stretcher-bearer was very marked. He organised reliefs of stretcher-bearers and led them into the shattered areas. Enemy snipers were very active in this section. This man was previously recommended for bravery in Messines Battle.

Pte. WILLIAM H. KLEVE, M.M.
For conspicuous bravery and devotion to duty at Dernancourt, S.W. of Albert, on 5th April, 1918, during an enemy attack. He was a member of a platoon post which accounted for over 400 dead in front of their post and kept the line intact. He carried supplies up to the riflemen and Lewis gunners and directed fire during the attack. The enemy had many machine-guns directed on our line, and when all N.C.O.'s and most of the men of his platoon had been casualties, he took charge and led a bombing party along a sap and drove enemy back. He personally accounted for many enemy, and considerably augmented his men's strength by his own splendid example. His gallantry was also conspicuous on several occasions between 27th March and 5th April. (Won with the 47th Battalion, A.I.F.).

Cpt. JOHN LEAHY, M.I.D.
For conspicuous services rendered.

Cpl. JOHN LEIGHTON, M.M.
For bravery and devotion to duty. On the 4th July, 1918, during the attack on Hamel, Corporal Leighton showed exemplary courage and devotion to duty while in charge of his signal section. Under heavy enemy fire he pushed forward with the leading wave, and was successful in immediately establishing communication with Battalion Headquarters. Throughout the whole operation, in spite of heavy enemy shell fire, he succeeded in keeping his lines intact and, although wounded, he refused to leave until his unit was relieved on the second day of the operation. By his conduct during the whole operation he set a splendid example to the other members of his section.

Lieut. CYRIL HARRINGTON GRIER LORIARD, M.C.
For conspicuous gallantry and devotion to duty when directing traffic under heavy shell fire. His great coolness and judgment had a marked influence at a time when excitement would have added to the danger and difficulties caused by heavy congestion on a narrow road.

DECORATIONS AWARDED THE FORTY-SECOND

2nd./Lieut. ADAM BRUCE MACKAY, M.C.
For conspicuous gallantry and devotion to duty when in charge of a support platoon during an attack. He successfully kept up communications between the various parties, promptly informing his C.O. of the different phases of the situation, quite heedless of enemy machine-gun fire at less than 50 yards.

L./Cpl. JOHN HENRY MANN, D.C.M., M.M.
For conspicuous gallantry and devotion to duty during operations north of Peronne on 31st August, 1918. In spite of heavy machine-gun fire, he brought his Lewis gun into action, firing from the hip. Later, when the enemy counter-attacked, he was surrounded on three sides, and, dismantling his gun, he fell back, sniping with his rifle, and established another post. M.M.: On 29th September, 1918, during operations South of Bony, Corporal Mann was in charge of a Lewis gun section. During an enemy counter-attack he rushed his gun to a favourable position and mounted it on a parapet. Standing in full view of the enemy, he engaged a number of machine-guns inflicting heavy casualties, and quickly gained superiority of fire, thus allowing our troops in the vicinity to get their heads up and bring fire to bear on the advancing enemy. His courageous action was undoubtedly of great assistance in repelling the enemy, and won the admiration of all ranks.

Sgt. FRANK WILLIAM MARRIAN, M.M.
On the 6/9/18 during operations East of Peronne, Sergeant Marrian handled his platoon magnificently—leading them forward to the objective with great skill and coolness, thereby saving many casualties, despite the extremely heavy enemy artillery and machine-gun fire. The valuable information which he collected, combined with his tactical handling of his command, was to a great extent, responsible for the success of the operation on his front. His conduct throughout the whole of the operation set a splendid example to all ranks, and inspired his men with the greatest confidence.

Pte. BENJAMIN MARSH, M.M.
On the 12/8/18, during operations on the Somme near Proyart, Private Marsh was employed as Company Runner, and carried out this responsible and dangerous work for many hours continuously. A heavily-shelled area had to be traversed on each occasion and Private Marsh's time for traversing the 2,000 yards of the direct route was 15 minutes. His plucky endurance and resolution were of material value in maintaining communication.

Pte. WILLIAM BARRON MIDGLEY, M.M.
For bravery in the Field.

Pte. ALEXANDER HENRY MOON, M.M.
For bravery in the Field.

Pte. GEORGE ROLAND MOORE, M.M.
On the 8/8/18, during the operations on the Somme, East of Hamel, Private Moore displayed splendid courage as a runner. During the advance on the enemy position he was entrusted with an important message. Although he had to pass through a heavy barrage of enemy shell fire and machine-gun fire, he did not hesitate and although he was wounded did not stop, and reached his destination and delivered the message. His courage and devotion to duty were of the highest order.

Sgt. GEORGE EVAN MORGAN, M.M. and Bar.

On 1/9/18, during operations North of Peronne, Sergeant Morgan displayed exceptional courage and initiative in the manner in which he handled his platoon. At one stage of the advance the platoon on his right was temporarily held up by the fire from a heavily manned German trench. Sergeant Morgan, realising the position, moved forward with Private Naylor and mopped up the trench concerned, by a rear and frontal attack. By this prompt action Sergeant Morgan undoubtedly saved us many casualties, and, in addition, made it possible for his flank platoon to advance on to the general line. Throughout the whole operation he maintained an attitude of courage and cheerfulness most inspiring to his men. Bar to M.M.: For conspicuous services rendered in the Field.

L./Cpl. SYDNEY ERSKINE MORRISON, M.M.

For bravery in the Field.

Major AUBREY CLYDE MOYES, M.C.

For conspicuous gallantry and devotion to duty. He successfully led his company through extremely heavy enemy barrage to the relief of a battalion, which he accomplished with a very few casualties, afterwards organising the defence with great skill, influencing his men by his personal example and courage. He displayed great resource and ability in keeping up communications with his headquarters even under the heaviest barrage, and he contributed largely to the successful holding of the line by his battalion.

L./Cpl. ROBERT MUNRO, M.M.

For bravery in the Field.

Lieut. KENNETH ADRIAN MURDOCH, M.I.D.

For conspicuous services.

L./Cpl. NORMAN STANLEY MURRAY, M.M.

On 1/9/18, during operations North of Peronne, this man's platoon suffered very heavy casualties from enemy machine-gun fire. On his Section Commander becoming a casualty, Private Murray assumed command and handled the section with the utmost intelligence and initiative, displaying great cheerfulness and courage, which served in very good stead to his badly knocked about comrades. On reaching the objective his keen observation and intelligent use of the ground were of invaluable assistance to his platoon commander.

T./Sgt. WILLIAM CARR McCASKER, M.M.

On the morning of July 31st, 1917, during an advance East of Messines, this N.C.O. was in charge of a platoon. His platoon was held up by machine-gun fire from a shell hole about 20 feet in front. In the attempt to rush the position, the platoon was stopped by wire, but the Corporal forced his way through alone. He threw a bomb into the garrison, killing two and wounding several, the remainder surrendering with their gun intact before the platoon arrived. His actions throughout were characterised by coolness, dash, and determination.

DECORATIONS AWARDED THE FORTY-SECOND 177

Pte. JOHN KISSOCK McDOWELL, M.M.

On 30th March, 1918, in Sailly le Sec, South of Albert, Private McDowell was engaged in preparing a hot meal for the troops in the trenches. His position was heavily shelled and his comrades sought shelter. This man continued to prepare the meal and make arrangements for its distribution, which owing to his devotion to duty and courage was possible even during the lulls in the enemy attack. His conduct was much admired by the men of his company, and it was only due to his example and fine soldierly bearing that the hot meal was able to be served to the troops immediately the enemy attack had been defeated. There was no officer or N.C.O. who could supervise this important duty, and his example to the other men of his kitchen is worthy of commendation.

Pte. DONALD ROY McGREGOR, M.M.

On the 6/9/18, during operations East of Peronne, whilst the platoon was advancing to its objective in the darkness through a swamp, Private McGregor who was carrying four magazines of Lewis gun ammunition, was wounded by enemy machine-gun fire through the wrist, unknown to the rest of the team. Despite the pain and weakness from loss of blood, he pushed forward on his own and at daylight sighted his section in action. Private McGregor advanced with the ammunition under heavy enemy machine-gun and rifle fire and reached the gun with ammunition intact. This enabled the gun to keep in action, and allowed the advance to continue. He went forward again with the platoon and refused to go to the dressing station until ordered to do so by his platoon officer. His conduct throughout the day won the admiration of all ranks.

Pte. THOMAS McGUIRE, M.I.D.

For conspicuous services rendered.

Driver DONALD McLAREN, M.M.

On 1/9/18, during operations North of Peronne, Driver McLaren was in charge of a pack mule carrying a hot meal to one of the front line companies. He was forced to travel by a different route to the remainder of the pack drivers, and carried out his task under the most adverse conditions. His route lay across a plateau in full view of the enemy and swept by enemy machine-gun fire and a continual target for searching fire from enemy artillery. He displayed great courage and tenacity of purpose in completing this task and his devotion to duty and his coolness whilst waiting the return of the dixies, was an example of soldierly spirit of the highest order.

Lieut. JOHN McLEAN, D.S.O., M.C., M.I.D.

On the afternoon of 5th April, 1918, at about 3 p.m., while at Sailly-le-Sec, Lieut. McLean saw two of the enemy entering the village of Bouzencourt, across the Somme River. He immediately set off with his runner, crossed the river and made fearlessly to Bouzencourt. He stalked the houses in which the enemy were seen and immediately charged the two Huns on lookout. He wounded one Hun with a revolver shot, and the other fired at him without result. Seizing his runner's rifle he then charged the Huns, who by this time had run. He overtook the wounded Hun bayoneted him, and then shot the other

Hun before he could return to his lines. This secured valuable identification. This officer has at all times shown conspicuous courage in face of the enemy. His action was witnessed by men of this brigade, and his courage and bravery in dealing with the enemy and securing such valuable information is much admired. D.S.O.: On 11-12th August, 1918, during operations on the Somme, he, with a Lewis gun section, attacked an enemy strong point north of Rosieres which was holding up the advance of a flank company, whose success meant the success of the line. With extraordinary gallantry he accounted for five enemy machine-guns, two by himself, cleared the strong point, and enabled the flank company to continue their advance. Just before reaching his final objective he was wounded, but continued to control his platoon until the capture of the final position, and then superintended consolidation. His magnificent example of courageous conduct produced a great moral effect on the whole of the attacking troops, and did much to insure his company's success. He did most splendid work. M.I.D.: For conspicuous services rendered.

Pte. AGESILAUS McWATTERS, M.M.

For bravery in the Field.

Pte. HERBERT ALFRED NAYLOR, M.M.

On 1/0/18, during operations North of Peronne, Private Naylor displayed a devotion to duty and splendid tenacity of purpose. He delivered a message from his Company Commander to the advancing platoons under extremely heavy machine-gun fire and artillery fire. Later, he materially assisted in the cutting off and the capture of a number of prisoners who were strongly defending a trench and interfering to a great extent with the advance of the platoon on the right. Throughout the operation his cheerfulness and courage were most marked.

L./Cpl. WILLIAM O'BRIEN, M.M.

For bravery in the Field.

Cpt. RICHARD DeB. F. O'BRYEN, M.I.D.

For conspicuous services rendered.

Lieut. WALTER LEONARD O'CONNOR, M.C. and M.M.

On the 12th August, 1918, during operations on the Somme near Proyart, this officer occupied a position some little distance in front of the main objective with the object of rushing two enemy machine-gun posts which were holding up another part of the line. He, with his platoon, successfully accomplished this, which greatly contributed to the success of the advance. A few minutes later a party of 80 enemy attempted to rush his platoon from the left. Lieut. O'Connor took a rifle from his runner, shot the officer, and directed one of his Lewis guns on to the party, completely disorganising and repelling the attack. His Company Commander was wounded some distance to his right, but despite a hail of enemy machine-gun bullets, he rushed to assist him, and was himself severely wounded in the attempt. M.M.: His initiative, courage and resource in dealing with surprise situations won the admiration of all who were working under and with him.

DECORATIONS AWARDED THE FORTY-SECOND

Lieut. ERIC EWEN PATERSON, M.C.

On 29th September, 1918, during operations south of Bony, he was sent forward to establish forward battalion headquarters. On meeting a strong enemy machine-gun post he immediately attacked it with his runners. Finding that the frontal attack had no effect, he rushed forward alone to a flank, and endeavoured to take the enemy in the rear, but was wounded before he attained his object. He displayed great gallantry and initiative.

Sgt. KENNETH GEORGE PATTERSON, M.M.

For bravery in the Field.

Lieut. JACK GRANT PATTISON, M.M.

On 6/9/18, during operations East of Peronne, Corporal Pattison who was in charge of the Scout Section, kept in constant touch with the enemy although continually exposed to heavy enemy machine-gun and rifle fire. He collected and passed back much information and was also of great assistance in keeping touch with our companies on the flanks. When his company's stretcher-bearers had become casualties he helped to attend to the wounded under exceptionally heavy shell fire at great personal risk. His courage and devotion to duty throughout the day were of the highest order and won the admiration of all ranks.

Sgt. JOHN CLARENCE PEACOCK, M.M.

On 29th September, 1918, during operations south of Bony, an enemy machine-gun was giving much trouble and had caused casualties to the members of Sergeant Peacock's platoon. This gun was situated on our left flank in rear of the trench we were occupying, and fired right down on our position. Sergeant Peacock locating this machine-gun took a Lewis gun, mounted it on the parapet although under direct fire of at least 5 enemy machine guns, brought fire to bear and put the hostile gun out of action. Later under cover of darkness, he crept forward and obtained identification of the enemy machine gunners. His courage and coolness undoubtedly saved his platoon from further casualties.

L./Cpl. JOHN THOMAS PETERS, M.M.

For conspicuous gallantry and devotion to duty during the period 16th September, 1918 to 11th November, 1918. This N.C.O. as leader of a Lewis gun section, on the 1st September, 1918, directed his section against two enemy machine-gun crews, putting them both out of action, and capturing their guns; thus enabling the rest of his platoon to advance. He has been present with the platoon since March, 1918, and has always led his section thoroughly and well, with utter disregard for personal safety, and always with a cheerful disposition.

Lieut. JAMES HENRY NORMAN PRICE, M.C., M.I.D.

On the night of 5th/6th June, in the trenches near Hill 63, Messines, this officer was in command of a raiding party against the enemy in U.15 a. Despite heavy enemy shelling of the approach and jumping off trenches, Second Lieut. Price assembled the storming party without loss, and at zero hour personally led the assault, which was pushed home with such vigour that the demoralised enemy garrison which greatly outnumbered the assaulting party, cast down their arms and fled through our own barrage to their support line. After inflicting heavy casualties and penetrating his communication trench as far as the support line, Second Lieut. Price skilfully withdrew the raiders through a hostile barrage to our own trenches. The personal courage displayed by this officer throughout this enterprise against the enemy inspired confidence and determination in his men. A total of 5 officers and 100 men took part in this raid.

L./Sgt. GEORGE JAMES HENRY READ, D.C.M., and M.M.

On 29th September, 1918, during operations south of Bony, while his platoon was bombing its way up the Hindenburg Line, he displayed great daring and initiative by covering the advance with a Lewis gun, and so allowed the party mopping up to continue their work of clearing out a machine-gun. From the trench in which his platoon was working he crept out in face of fire from six enemy machine guns, covered the enemy strong point from a distance of 40 yards, drew the fire, and thus prevented the enemy from firing on our bombers. This enabled them to get within range for bombing, and they cleared the strong point. M.M.: On 1/9/18, during operations North of Peronne T./Cpl. Read displayed great initiative and courage in the handling of his Lewis gun section. Perceiving that a flank platoon was being temporarily checked by enemy machine guns, he crept forward to a commanding position and at great personal risk observed the position of these guns. He then moved back to the platoon, took charge of his section and moved them to a flank where he successfully engaged and silenced the enemy guns. By his prompt action T./Corporal Read undoubtedly saved us many casualties and enabled the advance to be continued.

W.O. Cl., II. WILLIAM THOMAS REED, M.M. and Bar.

For conspicuous bravery and devotion to duty. On the 4th July, 1918, near Hamel, this N.C.O. displayed great bravery and devotion to duty during an attack on the enemy's position. During the final assault Sergeant Reed dashed ahead of his comrades, entered the enemy's trenches and attacked, singlehanded, a party of Germans, killing several, the remainder surrendering. He displayed much initiative and bravery during the consolidation of the new position, giving great assistance to his Company Commander in this work. During the whole operation, by his bravery and coolness and devotion to duty he set an excellent example to his men. Bar to M.M.: For bravery in the Field.

Pte. FREDERICK ROSE, M.M.

On the 8th August, 1918, during the operations on the Somme, East of Hamel, Private Rose displayed great daring throughout the whole of the advance, and by his bravery and resourcefulness was instrumental in capturing several prisoners. When the objective was reached he rendered valuable service as a Company Runner, having on several occasions to pass through heavy enemy machine-gun fire. By his bravery and high standard of devotion to duty he set a very fine example to his comrades.

Pte. ROBERT EDWIN RUTHERFORD, M.I.D.

For conspicuous services rendered.

DECORATIONS AWARDED THE FORTY-SECOND 181

Pte. PERCIVAL DOUGLAS SAVAGE, M.M.
On the 12th August, 1918, during the operations on the Somme near Proyart, Private Savage displayed splendid courage as a runner, and did exceptionally good work during the operation. Under most strenuous circumstances and heavy enemy artillery and machine-gun fire, this runner made four trips from the front line beyond Proyart to Battalion Headquarters, and also a number of shorter runs and succeeded in getting all messages through without delay.

Sgt. BERNARD SCANLAN, M.I.D.
For conspicuous services rendered.

Pte. HENRY SEPPLE, M.M.
During the operations East of Bray from the 22nd to the 26th August, 1918, inclusive, whilst employed as runner for his officer with the Battalion on our left flank, Private Sepple had to repeatedly come through heavy artillery and machine-gun barrage, particularly on the 22nd, when enemy counter-attacked, and again on 24th, when we attacked at mid-day, to deliver urgent and important messages, which he accomplished without delay. It is estimated that he made 30 trips from left flank to our Battalion. In addition, whilst running, he collected valuable and useful information en route from various sources, and, on the 22nd when the right flank Battalion of the English Division was retiring, he assisted his officer in rallying the men and inducing them to make a definite stand. Throughout the whole operations he displayed great coolness and daring.

Cpl. WILLIAM SHANKS, M.M.
For bravery in the Field.

Pte. CLARENCE LESLIE SMITH, M.M.
For conspicuously good work as a stretcher-bearer during October operations. He repeatedly went out to the most exposed position under intense artillery and machine-gun fire and attended to and brought in wounded to the R.A.P. He has acted as a stretcher-bearer during the operations from March to October, 1918, and has always carried out his duties without a thought of personal safety. On 12th August, 1918, North of Proyart, this man was most assiduous in bringing in wounded during a daylight attack. By his bravery and devotion to duty on this day, he was responsible for the saving of the lives of six men.

Lieut. ARTHUR FRED SNELLING, M.C.
On 31st August, 1918, during operations North of Peronne, this officer rushed two enemy machine guns which were holding up our advance, killing three of the crew, and taking the remainder prisoners. The second gun he put out of action by working up a shallow trench and bombing it. On reaching the enemy's main line of resistance, he organised and led a bombing party which was instrumental in killing many of the enemy, and capturing 20 prisoners. He then reorganised his platoon and established a definite line. Later, when the enemy attempted an outflanking movement on his company, he crawled forward with a few men and a Lewis gun and established a post from which he could enfilade the enemy and cause him severe casualties. He then crawled along the line under heavy fire, organised the supply of ammunition, and by his action enabled his men to hold and consolidate the position which they had captured.

Lieut. HURTLE ABEL ROY SQUIRES, M.I.D.
> For conspicuous services rendered.

L./Cpl. WILLIAM HENRY STAFFORD, M.M.
> For conspicuous gallantry in action and devotion to duty. On the night of 31st May, near Villers-Bretonneux, near Amiens, Private William Henry Stafford displayed remarkable courage in capturing a German patrol leader. Following a heavy bombardment a party of the enemy, consisting of one N.C.O. and ten men, rushed the Lewis gun outpost position of which Stafford was in charge; No. 2 of the gun was immediately stunned by a blow, leaving Stafford to fight three of the enemy singlehanded. He displayed great coolness and daring and succeeded in routing two of his opponents, capturing the third who was a German sergeant major, and he obtained identification of the enemy when it was urgently required. Throughout the whole operation he set an excellent example to his comrades.

Pte. ALBERT STAPLETON, M.M.
> On the 12th August, 1918, during operations on the Somme near Proyart, this man was advancing with a party on a strong point, when the No. 1 of the Lewis gun team became a casualty. He immediately took charge of the Lewis gun, and, firing from the hip, engaged a hostile machine-gun crew at 20 yards, thus preventing it swinging round on the rest of the party. His quickness and accuracy undoubtedly assisted in capturing the enemy garrison.

Pte. FRANK BELL STARK, M.M.
> For bravery in the Field.

Lieut. ERNEST McKENZIE STEVENSON, M.C.
> For conspicuous bravery and devotion to duty. On the 8th August, 1918, during the operations on the Somme, Lieut. E. M. Stevenson, who was acting as Battalion Scout Officer, located an enemy machine-gun post and dugout. Immediately opportunity offered he, accompanied by one N.C.O. rushed the machine-gun post and dugout and succeeded in capturing the gun and two officers and 40 other ranks. Lieut. Stevenson's daring action and exemplary courage had a very inspiring effect on all personnel under his command.

Cpt. ARTHUR PERCIVAL ST. JOHN, M.C.
> For bravery in the Field.

L./Cpl. WILLIAM JACK STUART, M.M.
> For bravery in the Field.

Pte. ARTHUR EDWARD SUMMERS, M.M.
> For bravery in the Field.

L./Cpl. EMILE AUGUSTA TARDENT, M.M.
> On the 12/8/18, during operations on the Somme near Proyart, this N.C.O. showed great skill in dealing with hostile machine-guns. He directed the tactics of his own and adjoining sections in clearing up difficult machine-gun posts. On one occasion, in order to complete an outflanking movement of another section, which he himself directed, he rushed the post, accomplished the object, but was severely wounded. His daring action and exemplary courage had a very inspiring effect on all personnel under his command.

Lieut. JULES LOUIS TARDENT, C. de G. (French).
For conspicuous services rendered.

Pte. ERIC THOMPSON, M.M.
On 31st July, 1917, East of Messines, this man showed great courage and coolness in the offensive. He was deputed to carry a message from one post to another and on to Company Headquarters, through intense enemy barrage. The enemy was observed massing for attack opposite the one post where the S O S Rockets had been destroyed by rain. This concentration could not be seen from the second post, and signal communication had been cut. The promptness with which this man got his message through, helped very largely to save the situation.

Sgt. JOHN ELLIS THOMPSON, M.M.
On 29th September, 1918, during operations South of Bony, when approaching the Hindenburg Line, Sergeant Thompson's Platoon Commander became a casualty. Sergeant Thompson immediately took charge of the platoon and reorganised the men who had become scattered owing to the heavy enemy shell fire. He then led them on, and took up his position with his company. Later at Malakoff he again showed great ability and leadership in bringing his platoon through heavy machine-gun and artillery fire and dug in near the Hindenburg Line. His courage and coolness under fire set a splendid example to his men.

Pte. COLIN THOMSEN, M.M.
For bravery in the Field.

Cpt. EWING GEORGE THOMSON, M.C.
For bravery and devotion to duty. On the morning of the 24th April, in the vicinity of Heilly—near Albert—Captain Ewing George Thomson, R.M.O., tended the wounded in the open from 4 a.m. till 11 a.m. During this period he was subjected to very heavy shelling between the hours of 4 a.m. and 7 a.m., but he remained continuously at the Aid Post and worked with great devotion and courage throughout the day, although suffering from the effects of gas contracted almost at the commencement of the bombardment. His rapidity in evacuating the wounded from the gassed area was no doubt responsible for the preservation of many valuable lives. This officer personally assisted to remove wounded men under extremely heavy shell fire to places of safety, carrying out his duties for considerable periods whilst wearing his gas mask. His bravery and devotion was the admiration of the whole Battalion.

Sgt. CLAIR ERQHART THOW, M.M.
For bravery in the Field.

Lieut. THOMAS DESMOND TIERNEY, D.C.M.
For conspicuous gallantry and devotion to duty. He performed invaluable service in the handling of his Lewis guns, which were some distance apart, at a critical period, and under heavy fire.

Pte. ARTHUR TOOMEY, M.M.
For bravery in the Field.

W.O. Cl., 2 SAMUEL WILLIAM TOOTH, D.C.M.

On the 8th August, 1918, during the operation on the Somme, East of Hamel, Sergeant Major Tooth showed conspicuous courage, coolness, and initiative throughout the whole advance. On one occasion when the right flank was held up by enemy machine-gun fire, he organised a small party of men who were in the immediate vicinity, outflanked the machine-gun positions, and killed or captured the whole crews, then mopped two large dugouts nearby, accounting for two officers and 40 other ranks His conduct during the whole operation was a splendid example of courage and devotion to duty.

Lieut. CLARENCE SAMUEL TRUDGIAN, M.C.

On 31st August, 1918, during operations North of Peronne, when his company was hung up in an attack on a strong enemy position, T./Captain Trudgian fearlessly exposed himself by walking along the front encouraging his men under heavy machine gun fire at short range and in front of a battery of field guns firing with open sights. He led his men forward and captured the position, taking many machine-guns, the crews of which were killed at their posts. T./Captain Trudgian reorganised his depleted platoons, and when the enemy counter-attacked in force he succeeded in beating them off and retaining an important tactical position. The greater part of the success of the operation was due to the manner in which this officer dealt with a critical situation.

Cpl. CECIL DARCY TWEED, M.M.

On 1/9/18, during operations North of Peronne, T./Corporal Tweed's platoon was in support. At one stage of the advance he observed a gap between two of the leading platoons and immediately, on his own initiative moved his section forward to fill it. He successfully mopped up the area accounting for two machine-guns and numerous prisoners, and maintained touch between the two platoons. By his prompt action T./Cpl. Tweed undoubtedly saved us numerous casualties, and his clever handling of his section enabled him to perform the task with no casualties in his section.

Sgt. DONALD WILLIAM WALKER, D.C.M.

For conspicuous gallantry and devotion to duty in organising a party, leading them to an attack on a machine-gun that was giving trouble, capturing the gun, killing three of the enemy, and taking ten prisoners. When his platoon officer became a casualty, he took command of his platoon for two days under most adverse conditions.

T./Cpt. STANLEY RICHARD WARRY, M.C.

On the 12th August, 1918, during operations on the Somme, near Proyart, Lieutenant Warry commanded a company with gallantry and initiative, reaching his objective with exceedingly few casualties although the enemy were in strength against him, opposing him with heavy machine-gun fire. During the advance he was subjected to severe artillery fire, and bombed by hostile aircraft. He kept a constant stream of reliable and valuable information sent to his Battalion Headquarters. His excellent command of his company contributed greatly to the success of the operation.

DECORATIONS AWARDED THE FORTY-SECOND

Pte. WILLIAM GEORGE WATSON, M.M.
For bravery in the Field.

Pte. JOHN FENWICK WEATHERED, M.M.
On 6/9/18, during operations East of Peronne, Private Weathered's platoon came under heavy enemy fire and several casualties were caused. As some stretcher-bearers were included in these casualties, Private Weathered volunteered to act as stretcher-bearer, and in spite of heavy enemy shell fire, dressed the wounded and helped to carry out regardless of his own safety. Although continually exposed to the enemy fire he carried out his self-imposed task in a cool and courageous manner which won the admiration of all ranks.

Sgt. JOSEPH WALTER WEBSTER, M.M.
On the 8/8/18, during the operations on the Somme, East of Hamel, Sergeant Webster displayed great gallantry and leadership. During the advance through dense fog and in spite of heavy flank machine-gun fire from the direction of Chipilly, he fought his platoon to its final objective, mopping up many dugouts on his way.

L./Cpl. NORMAN WILLIAMS, M.M.
For bravery in the Field.

Pte. JOHN HENRY WILLS, M.M.
For bravery in the Field.

Pte. FRANK WILSON, D.C.M.
For conspicuous courage and devotion to duty. At about 5 p.m. on afternoon 30th March, 1918, North of Sailly-le-Sec, near Albert, Private Frank Wilson volunteered to carry a message to Battalion Headquarters, having to pass through several bands of fire of advance enemy machine-guns. He was wounded severely, in the back and was unable to rise, but crawled on over open ground, sniped at by enemy snipers, and in spite of his great pain and the great danger, struggled on until he delivered his message. This soldier carried out his duty in a way that has geen greatly admired by all his comrades and set such an example of courage and devotion to duty that is worthy of the highest praise.

W.O. Cl. 2. STANLEY WILSON, D.C.M.
For conspicuous gallantry and devotion to duty. He organised working and carrying parties with great skill and coolness under fire. He commanded a platoon when his officer became a casualty, and on many occasions showed splendid courage and determination.

Pte. CLINTON JAMES NICHOLSON WINKS, M.M.
On 6/9/18, during operations East of Peronne, Private Winks acted as C.S. Bearer. When his company was heavily shelled and other stretcher-bearers had become casualties, he attended to the wounded under heavy shell fire, fearlessly exposing himself in the course of his duties. He then organised a party of stretcher-bearers and succeeded in evacuating all the wounded under extremely adverse circumstances. By his courage and steadfast devotion to duty, Private Winks set a fine example to all ranks.

Lieut. JOHN FREDERICK WOOD, M.C.

For conspicuous gallantry and devotion to duty. He volunteered to take out a patrol, and penetrating some distance into enemy territory, examined dugouts and pill boxes. On the following evening he again took a patrol some 300 yards beyond our front, although enemy snipers had already caused several casualties.

Lieut.-Col. ARTHUR RAFF WOOLCOCK, D.S.O., M.I.D., C. de. G. (French).

For distinguished services in the Field. M.I.D. (2): Deserving of special mention. C. de G.: For conspicuous services rendered.

Pte. WILLIAM WRIGHT, M.M.

For bravery in the Field.

Pte. ROBERT YARWOOD, M.M. (A.A.M.C. Attached).

On April 5th, 1918, he was a stretcher-bearer working at a R.A.P. at Buire near Albert, on the Ancre River. He was a source of inspiration to all his fellow stretcher-bearers, was tireless in his work, was cheerful and courageous under very trying circumstances, and volunteered again and again to carry out wounded men to the evacuating point. He made many journeys during the day between Buire and Ribemont, the loading post, under harassing shell fire, and by his example encouraged and sustained the other bearers.

Cpt. ERNEST YELLAND, M.I.D.

For conspicuous services rendered.

MEMORIES REVIVED

Reading the foregoing pages has reawakened personal experiences herewith recorded by

Name..

Rank–Company...

Date...

MEMORIES REVIVED

MEMORIES REVIVED

MEMORIES REVIVED

MEMORIES REVIVED

MEMORIES REVIVED

Wholly set up and printed in Australia
by
W. R. SMITH & PATERSON PTY. LTD.,
Marshall Street, The Valley,
Brisbane, Australia.
1938.

www.ingramcontent.com/pod-product-compliance
Lightning Source LLC
Chambersburg PA
CBHW031142160426
43193CB00008B/226